LEARNING C SHELL SCRIPTING GENTLY

Sujata Biswas

Copyright © 2017 Sujata Biswas

All rights reserved.

Content

Introduction

Why should I learn C shell (csh) shell scripting?

  Prerequisites

  The infrastructure used to create this book

Chapter 1: What is a Shell?

  Finding out your Shell

Chapter 2: Fundamentals of Shell

  Streams

  Redirection

  Variables

Chapter 3: C shell (csh) Essentials

  Redirection of the Error stream

  Command combinations

    AND operator &&

    OR operator ||

  Single and double quotes backslash and backticks

  Command substitution in C shell

Chapter 4: C Shell User Customization

  The .login and .cshrc files for personal customization.

  The csh.login and csh.cshrc file for System Wide Customization

Chapter 5: Regular expressions and grep, sed, find and awk

  Meta Characters

  Grep Command

  The sed command

    The -n and p command of sed

    Deletion using sed "d" command

    Adding a line using sed's a command
  The find command
  The awk command
    Syntax of awk
    Examples of awk
    A note about the buffers
    Using Selection conditions in awk
    $NF and other variables in awk
    Simple formatting
    Combining commands
    Awk Blocks
Chapter 6: Advanced take on Shell Fundamentals
  Variables
    User-created variables
    Existing or Predefined Variables
    Environmental Variables
  Aliases
  Various options of echo command
    The \b character code - backspace
    The -n syntax – no new line
    The tab \t character code:
    The form feed \f character code
    The vertical tab \v character code:
  Exit command
  Reading from the command line
  Positional Parameters in C Shell
  Operators and their types
    Arithmetical operators
    Relational operators
    File testing operators
    Logical Operators

Chapter 7: Beginning C Shell Scripting
  If-then-else: Decision Making
    Supported Syntaxes of If-Then-Else
  Putting command outputs inside variables using back ticks
  Scripts
  Switch-Case Decision
  Looping
    While looping
    Foreach looping
Chapter 8: Advanced Techniques and Scripting in C shell
  Break and Continue command:
  Repeat looping:
  Parameters Again:
    Script name Identifier $0
    Parameter counter $#argv
    Parameter lister $argv
  Shift command
  Introducing Arrays
Chapter 9 Frequently Asked Questions
  What is the difference between using source command and executing a script normally?
  How can I initiate an infinite loop using "while" in BASH and C shells?
  What is the significance of exit 1, exit 2 and exit 3 etc. in the shell scripts?
  How do I control and validate input of arguments to the script?
  How do I troubleshoot my C shell scripts?
  Is it possible to accomplish file parsing in C shell scripts?

INTRODUCTION

Welcome and Thank you for buying Learning C Shell Scripting Gently. The endeavor of this book is to cover the nitty-gritty of C shell environment before putting your attention into creating scripts in C shell. All the components needed to fire your shell scripts will be covered.

WHY SHOULD I LEARN C SHELL (CSH) SHELL SCRIPTING?

Bill Joy developed the C shell at the University of California, Berkeley. He is also famous for founding the company called Sun Microsystems (eventually bought by Oracle).

You can find many resources on BASH scripting, but scarcely anything on C shell scripting. This book is an attempt to fill this gap. While BASH scripting, is, no doubt, popular and widely used in many a vertical. C shell scripting has created a niche of its own. It is the de facto shell in engineering companies. It is also used in Universities due to its "resemblance" to the programming language C. In my opinion, it is a skill that you ought to have in your resume for the differential it creates. It can also be a precursor to learning the C language and then proceed to popular languages such as Java and JavaScript and Python.

Most of the engineering firms employ, obviously, engineers and these days nearly everyone has access to Operating Systems such as Ubuntu, Fedora or Centos. So, the knowledge level of users has dramatically risen over the years. I am sure you wouldn't like to be a System Administrator who merely knows the Supervisor's password, would you? So, it is imperative that you update your knowledge periodically.

PREREQUISITES

You must have some knowledge of any Linux Operating Systems. If you haven't got the requisite experience, please go for a learning course on Basic Linux Operating Systems and work at least for a month or two. That should be enough. Those who have experience working in Linux can skip the First Section, though it is not recommended.

THE INFRASTRUCTURE USED TO CREATE THIS BOOK

Virtual VM Virtual Box on Windows 10 Machine with Ubuntu and Centos Installation.

Accessing Ubuntu and Centos using Putty for Windows.

CHAPTER 1: WHAT IS A SHELL?

A shell is an interface between you, the user, and the system. This is a simplistic definition of a shell. It is a command interpreter as well. The shell translates the commands you enter in the shell to a language understandable to the system. Here, the system refers to the kernel. The kernel is the heart of the Linux Operating system, in fact, the kernel is the Linux operating system itself. So, the shell coordinates with the kernel to get the commands you enter to be executed. The Kernel itself provides an abstraction layer between the you, the user, and the hardware components of your computer through drivers. The relation is illustrated in the following screenshot.

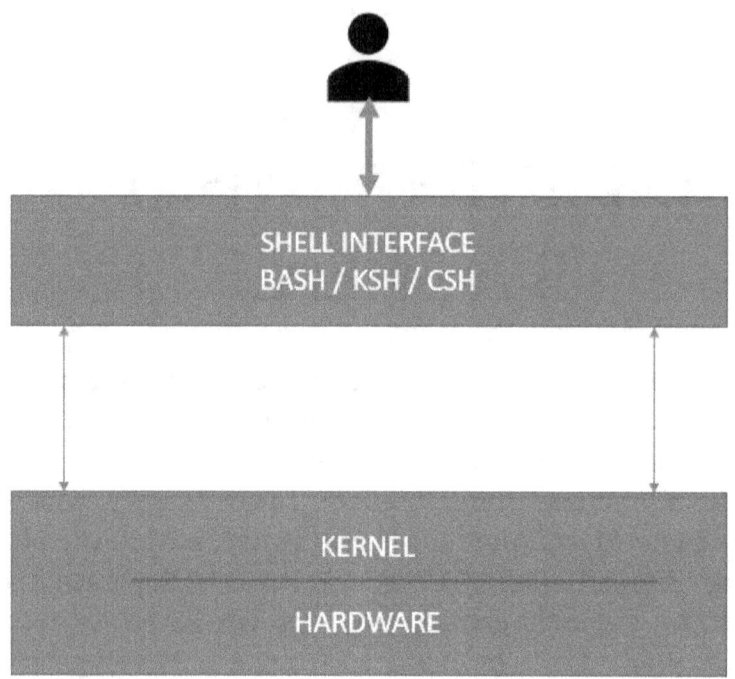

The shell also offers programming abilities. If you are coming from the Windows background, you will understand the role of **cmd** (command interpreter) and DOS batch programming. Similarly, the

equivalent of DOS batch programming is Shell Programming in Linux distributions. The shell script is nothing but an ASCII (text) file that has series of control or decision structures with the commands you use on the Command line. The three main shells are BASH, Korn and C shell. Obviously, the BASH (Bourne again Shell) and Korn shells are very popular worldwide, while C shell has a niche market in, mostly, engineering firms.

FINDING OUT YOUR SHELL

To find the shell you are using, login to a Linux distribution of your choice. Enter your credentials, that is your login name and password and you will see the prompt:

$

Note: In this book, examples are from Ubuntu and some from Centos as well.

To check if the shell is the C-Shell or **csh**, enter the following command on the prompt. The echo command displays the value of the variable **SHELL**. The **SHELL** is a pre-configured variable. Since it is a variable $ sign must precede it.

$ echo $SHELL

The value we get is:

$ echo $SHELL
/bin/bash

This is not what you are looking for. You want to see the absolute path to the C shell executable. To go to C shell, type **csh**

$ csh

The prompt changes to the C shell prompt:

%

% echo $SHELL

% /bin/bash

However, the value of **SHELL** variable remains unchanged, because it is the parent shell. It can be called the grandfather shell as well, depending on how many shells you have traversed through. So, it is always better to use a login name that has been created with C shell. It is possible that C shell or **csh** is not installed in your Operating System.

To install the **C- shell** or **csh**, enter the following command, login to existing shell **bash** or **ksh**:

$ sudo apt install csh

Note: The command is for the Ubuntu Operating system.

Note: In Centos, the command to install C shell:

 # yum install csh

After the installation of the csh shell, create a user using the following command. Since, Ubuntu has no root account, you should **sudo** from your current shell to elevate and use the **adduser** command.

Here is the process using the **adduser** command along with the username. Do not give the username in title case.

$ sudo adduser jeff

Adding user `jeff'...

Adding new group `jeff' (1005)...

Adding new user `jeff' (1005) with group `jeff'...

Creating home directory `/home/jeff'...

Copying files from `/etc/skel'...

Enter new UNIX password:

Retype new UNIX password:

passwd: password updated successfully

Changing the user information for jeff

Enter the new value, or press ENTER for the default

    Full Name []: **Jeff Smith**

    Room Number []: **102**

    Work Phone []: **000000**

    Home Phone []: **000001**

    Other []:

Is the information correct? [Y/n] **Y**

However, the user that is created, by default, has bash shell. What you can do is edit the **/etc/passwd** file directly using your favorite editor:

$ sudo nano /etc/passwd

Change the line from:

jeff:x:1005:1005:Jeff Smith,102,000000,000001:/home/jeff:/bin/**bash**

To

jeff:x:1005:1005:Jeff Smith,102,000000,000001:/home/jeff:/bin/**csh**

Note: You just need to change the shell from **/bin/bash** to **/bin/csh**. Do not try this at your work location. Also, note, that this is a hack. The **passwd** file is the repository of users' information in your system. There is a command called **passwd** as well. So, don't get confused between the file passwd and command passwd.

Login as jeff:

Check the value of $SHELL variable

% echo $SHELL

/bin/csh

%

Let's try creating a user that defaults to the csh shell. The following command will do the trick on Centos.

$ useradd -d /home/jeff -s /bin/csh jeff

After changing the password using the **passwd** command, try logging into the shell. Perform **echo $SHELL** to verify the shell you are in.

Note: You can also use the **chsh** command to change your shell and logout and login back. If currently you have bash shell, then you can change the shell to **csh** (In Ubuntu, you have to install C shell).

Step1: Shows the current shell

$ echo $SHELL

/bin/bash

Step2: Run the **chsh** command, asks for the password and path to the C shell – which /bin/csh

$ chsh

Changing shell for jeff.

Password:

New shell [/bin/bash]: /bin/csh

Shell changed.

$

Step3: Login back and check the shell:

$ echo $SHELL

/bin/csh

CHAPTER 2: FUNDAMENTALS OF SHELL

STREAMS

Linux / Unix operating systems offer three streams. Streams are channels of communications between the input command that you type from the keyboard and its resulting outputs that you see on your display monitor. The outputs are of two types: standard and error outputs. The Operating Systems assigns each stream a file descriptor that you can see in the following table:

Note: A file descriptor is a handle or a number that is assigned by the Operating Systems.

Streams	File Descriptor	Symbol	Device Associated
Standard Input	0	<	Keyboard
Standard Output	1	>	Monitor or a file
Standard Error	2	2>	Monitor or a file

Table A

REDIRECTION

This topic is associated with streams. Redirection allows you to change the standard preassigned device associated with standard input and standard output. For example, instead of feeding the command with what you type, you can redirect the content of a file in standard input stream to command. Or instead of displaying standard output on your monitor, you can "redirect" the output of the **who** command to a file.

For instance:

$ who > userlist.txt

The output of the command is redirected using the greater than symbol > to a file called **userlist.txt**. Opening **userlist.txt**:

$ who -u > userlist.txt

$ cat userlist.txt

jeff   pts/1   2017-06-22 00:48 .   20866 (192.168.1.5)

You can redirect standard input to a command. This is best illustrated by using the Linux's sort command. If you enter

$ info sort

You will find that it is used for manipulating standard input stream and display it on your monitor. Consider this file, containing the results of a class test:

$ cat classtest

19

Jerry 40

Mary 78

Peter 89

Jo 72

Jeff 89

Ann 56

Victor 80

Bob 43

Earl 20

Park 90

If you redirect the content of this file as an input stream to **sort**, the command will sort the result in the alphabetical order:

$ sort < classtest
Ann 56
Bob 43
Earl 20
Jeff 89
Jerry 40
Jo 72
Mary 78
Park 90
Peter 89
Victor 80

A pictorial representation of standard input and output streams is as follows:

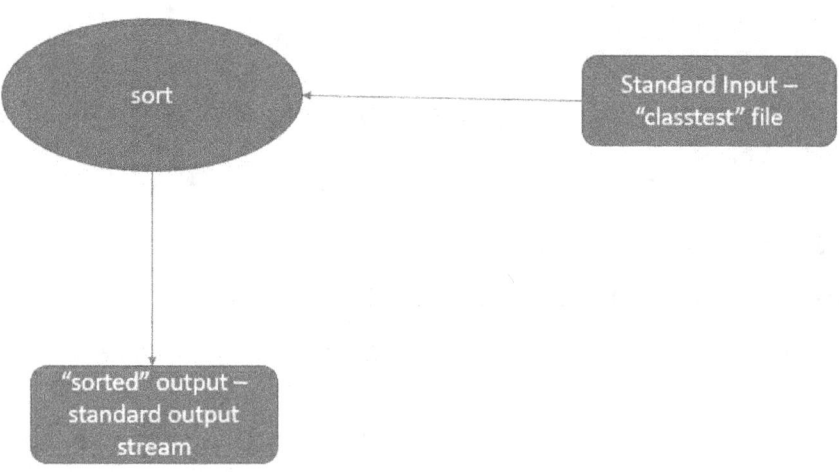

Note: While Standard error is supported in Bash shell it is not supported in the C shell.

Redirecting the error **2>** in csh shell, note, **hello1** is a file that doesn't exist.

$ ls hello1 2> stanerror

ls: cannot access hello1: No such file or directory

ls: cannot access 2: No such file or directory

If you run the same command in Bash shell, just type **bash** in your prompt to travel to bash environment:

$ bash

In, Bash shell, the Standard error is redirected to a file called **stanerror**

$ ls hello1 2> stanerror

Displaying the content of the stanerror file

$ cat stanerror

ls: cannot access 'hello1': No such file or directory

VARIABLES

A variable is a location in the memory of your system that store/hold values. They are two parts of a variable, its name and its value. The variable name cannot start with a numeric. There are two types of variables, user and system (or predefined) variables.

The user variables are defined by you. The syntax in the **C shell** differs from the **Bash**:

1) Define a variable that is applicable to the "current" shell only using the set command. This command accepts spaces between the assignment =

$ set hi = hello

$ echo $hi

hello

What does it mean that it only applies to the current shell?

Open another instance of the shell by typing C shell again

$ set hi = hello

$ echo $hi

hello

Here, you type C shell again to open another shell.

$ csh

$ echo $hi

hi: Undefined variable.

So, you can infer that the variable "hi" is not inherited when another instance of the **C shell** is opened. Thus, it is called a local variable. If you want to have another instance of the shell inherit the value of a variable, then you should define the variable using the **setenv** command. That variable is called an environmental global variable. Unlike, set command, **setenv** doesn't use = to assign a value. A space will do.

Step1: Define a Global Variable called "Hey" and value it to Hello

$ setenv HEY hello

Step2: Check the value of variable HEY

$ echo $HEY

hello

Step3: Open another instance of the csh shell

$ csh

Step4: Again, check the value of HEY

$ echo $HEY

hello

Tip: What is this another instance of the **csh** command? How do I see it? You see it simply by entering the command that looks at the processes, the option that you should use is **-u** for that user:

$ ps -u jeff

  PID TTY   TIME CMD

23361 ?   00:00:00 sshd

23362 pts/1 00:00:00 csh #Default instance of csh

23404 pts/1 00:00:00 csh #Another instance of csh

23456 pts/1 00:00:00 ps

Note: Conventionally, Global Variables set by the **setenv** command should be in Capital letters.

Variables will be (and must be) covered more extensively in this book.

CHAPTER 3: C SHELL (CSH) ESSENTIALS

As you know development of C shell took place at the University of California under the aegis of Bill Joy. He also developed the text editor **VI**.

The C shell is an interactive environment and a scripting/programming language. Before diving into scripting, you should know the essential components of the C shell. This will help you create a solid foundation. Without knowing essentials and commands such as **grep, find, cut, sed and awk**, your shell scripts will not be successful.

In the C Shell essentials, you will learn about the following topics:

- Redirection of the error stream
- Command combinations
- Difference between single and double quotes and backticks
- Command substitution in C shell
- Exit Status

REDIRECTION OF THE ERROR STREAM

You know that standard error stream redirection is different from the Bash shell. The **csh** doesn't support **2>** . The following operators are used **>&** and **>>&** to redirect the error stream to a file.

Step1: Performing **ls -l** on a non-existent file **nofile.txt** and the resulting error message is

$ ls -l nofile.txt

ls: cannot access nofile.txt: No such file or directory

Step2: Redirecting the error stream to a file named **errorstore.txt**; we don't see the error message anymore

$ ls -l nofile.txt >& errorstore.txt

$

Step3: Opening the file errorstore.txt, which shows that it has consumed the error message.

$ cat errorstore.txt

ls: cannot access nofile.txt: No such file or directory

If you wish to append error information to the same file, in this case, **errorstore.txt**, then use **>>&**

My personal experience has been that people use the command tee for convenience. We will see how. For quick guidance on **tee** command, enter

$ info tee

Usage:

Step1: The following command shows the contents of Jeff's directory:

$ ls

classtest errorstore.txt hello list.txt stanerror tmp.file userlist.txt

Step2: we can redirect the output to a list, say, list.txt, using the redirect symbol >.

$ ls > list.txt

Step3: Demonstrates the usefulness of the tee command, using the pipe | operator. The command **tee** sends the standard output to two entities, to a file and to the standard display as well.

$ ls | tee list2.txt

$ ls | tee list2.txt

classtest
errorstore.txt
hello
list.txt
stanerror
tmp.file
userlist.txt

Note: The Pipe | is an operator that saves the output of the first command in a buffer while presenting it as an input to the second command.

COMMAND COMBINATIONS

C shell supports command sequencing, where two disparate commands are combined. Unlike pipe or other operators like && (AND) and || (OR), these commands are independent of each other, there is no connection between the commands. For example:

$ date ; uptime

Sat Jun 24 16:49:38 IST 2017

16:49:38 up 7 days, 56 min, 4 users, load average: 0.00, 0.01, 0.00

You can group the commands as well and redirect the output to a single file, this is such a time saver, three commands are put inside a parenthesis and redirected to a single file uptime.txt

$ (date ; uptime ; ls) > uptime.txt

$ cat uptime.txt

Sat Jun 24 16:54:07 IST 2017

16:54:07 up 7 days, 1:00, 4 users, load average: 0.00, 0.00, 0.00

classtest
errorstore.txt

hello
list2.txt
list.txt
stanerror
tmp.file
uptime.txt
userlist.txt

Another way of combining commands is using conditional operators **AND** and **OR**. It is important to study these operators as they used in shell scripting a lot. Used both in Bash and C shell environments.

AND operator &&

The first command must be successful for the second command to execute. Otherwise the AND conditional fails:

first_command_success && second_command_executes

Example of success:

$ ls hello && uptime

hello

17:02:28 up 7 days, 1:09, 3 users, load average: 0.00, 0.00, 0.00

Example of failure:

Performing ls on a non-existent file called hello1.

$ ls hello1 && uptime

ls: cannot access hello1: No such file or directory

As you can see, the failure of first command stops the conditional on the track.

OR OPERATOR ||

The first command must fail for the second command to succeed.

first_command_fails || second_command_executes

The following example, deliberately performs **ls** on a file that does not exist to execute the second command.

$ ls hello1 || uptime

ls: cannot access hello1: No such file or directory

17:05:43 up 7 days, 1:12, 3 users, load average: 0.00, 0.00, 0.00

SINGLE AND DOUBLE QUOTES BACKSLASH AND BACKTICKS

Single quotes are powerful, as they maintain the sanctity of the string enclosed. They can prevent variable expansion effectively. Double quotes also remove the special meaning of metacharacters (like | pipe) apart from dollar $ preceding a variable. The double quote will allow the variable expansion, this is because though double quotes will eliminate the special meaning of some metacharacters, it allows $ sign to expand to its value.

Consider the example below:

Step1: Set a value for the variable "a"

$ set a = 50

Step2: Checking the value of the variable

$ echo $a

50

Step3: Using double quotes, which allows variable expansion.

$ echo "The price of 1 pound meat is $a Dollars! "

The price of 1 pound meat is 50 Dollars!

Step4: Using single quotes, variable $a holds no special meaning now, the variable expansion is stopped. The result of echo is literal:

$ echo 'The price of 1 pound meat is $a Dollars! '

The price of 1 pound meat is $a Dollars!

Double Quotes preserving whitespaces:

This aspect of double quotes is often ignored, look at the following example without double quotes. The echo command has ignored the long whitespace between Hello and how are you

$ echo Hello   how are you
Hello how are you

Here, double quotes come to rescue, note the difference:

$ echo "Hello   how are you"
Hello   how are you

This is how double quotes preserve the whitespace.

In Linux, certain special characters like a question mark, brackets, > (greater than), < (less than) and the hyphen is treated differently by the shell. Such characters are called metacharacters and this is, of course, tied up with Regular expressions. Backslash is also a metacharacter. Backslash strips off meaning of some special characters. Remember that > is both used as "less than" in shell scripting for making numerical comparisons and as a redirection operator when used in commands. But when such metacharacters are used with **echo** command, the shell is confused how to treat them.

$ echo >
Missing name for redirect.

$ echo >>
Missing name for redirect.

$ echo ?
echo: No match.

$ echo *
examples.desktop stanerror

$ echo []
echo: No match.

Applying the backslash on the previous command results in a different output:

$ echo \>
>

$ echo \>>
Missing name for redirect.

$ echo \>\>
>>

Note: Here you need two backslashes to negate the special meaning of >>, which is the append mechanism.

$ echo \?
?

$ echo *
*

$ echo \[]
[]

Of course, you can achieve the same results using double and single quotes. Backslashes have significant application in pattern matching and filtering commands such as **sed** and **awk**. Some complex **sed** structure may contain large numbers of backslashes and it can get very confusing to even experienced eyes.

Another usage of backslash is in long command structures that have multiple lines, here backslash is used to stop the end of the line.

COMMAND SUBSTITUTION IN C SHELL

Command substitution is where the Linux command's output is turned into a string. A string is an order of alphanumeric characters that can be manipulated by other commands so that they can be used in Shell scripts to test TRUE or FALSE conditions and pattern matching.

Whereas Bash shell supports both constructs using parentheses and backticks, C shell only supports backticks.

As noted earlier, a variable is given a value from a command's output. For instance, the output of **the ls command** is

This is an example from the BASH shell:

$ ls

hello1 hello2

Command substitution is merely, here a variable called Greetings is given the value of the ls command:

$ Greetings=$ (ls)

$ echo $Greetings

hello1 hello2

What happens if we try the same commands and the parenthesis construct in the C shell?

Step1: So far so good.
$ ls
hello1 hello2

Step2: You get an error. Do not be afraid of errors. When you are learning something new, and you get errors and try to resolve them, you will learn faster in the long run.

$ set Greetings = $ (ls)
Illegal variable name.

Step3: Using backticks: Now, this is successful.

$ set Greetings = `ls`

$ echo $Greetings

hello1 hello2

CHAPTER 4: C SHELL USER CUSTOMIZATION

C shell, like the bash shell uses startup files to customize their users' environment. This customization is of two types, one that is applicable to all users and another for a specific user. The former is called system-wide customization, and while the latter is personal customization. The **etc** directory is the repository of the system-wide customization files, while a user's personal HOME directory is where her/his/their customization files reside.

The system-wide customization files are:

- **csh.login**
- **csh.cshrc**

The personal customization files for C shell are:

- **.login**
- **.cshrc**
- **.logout**

Note: The customization files start with a period and seen using with **ls -a** command.

The .login and .cshrc files for personal customization.

Both the files are read when you login to the shell. But when it is a non-login shell, only **.cshrc** is executed. The **.cshrc** file is the environment file for customization, while the **.login** is the shell file for customization.

Create **.cshrc** file and the **.login** files in /home/pratim's directory

$ cat .cshrc

echo " The hostname is `hostname` "

$ cat .login

echo "Hello today's date is `date` "

Save the files and login in using putty or whatever terminal emulator you have:

This is an example of a login shell:

login as: pratim
pratim@192.168.1.4's password:
Last login: Fri Jun 30 01:25:26 2017 from 192.168.1.2
The hostname is centos.localhost.localdomain
Hello today 's date is Fri Jun 30 01:31:55 IST 2017

As you can see, both the files were executed.

Example of a non-login shell, if you are already logged in as another user, **jeff** and login to **pratim** using the **su** command:

Step:1 Check that you are logged in as another user
[jeff@centos ~]$ whoami
jeff
Step2: Use the su command to switch user to **pratim** from **jeff**
[jeff@centos ~]$ su pratim
Password:
The hostname is centos.localhost.localdomain
[pratim@centos jeff]$

After you enter the password, only pratim's **.cshrc** is executed. This is called an environment file for the shell. **The local shell file .login is NOT executed in a non-login shell.** In real life, IT folks use the **.cshrc** file to provide personal customization. In fact, it is nothing fancy, just some software hierarchies in the PATH variable.

Login shells are when you login to the shell and your credentials (username and password) are checked against a database – which can be as simple as the **/etc/passwd file**, to a major LDAP/Active Directory structure to even remote infrastructure on Cloud. While non-login shells do not require such authentication.

Perhaps, a simpler example is needed to explain the difference between **login** and **non-login** shells.

To rehash:

.login has the following code; the date command is enclosed in backticks so that it expands to its standard output.

echo "Hello today 's date is `date` "

Important Note: The double quotes DO NOT have any effect on backticks, however, if you were to use single quotes, the `date` will not expand, the string will become literal. Please try this example, as you will quickly forget something as fundamental as this.

On the other hand, **.cshrc** has this piece of code added:

echo " The hostname is `hostname` "

Test:
1) Log in as "jeff"
2) Enter the password:

You can see that following execution of both **.login** and .cshrc personal/startup/initialization/ customization files.

login as: jeff

jeff@192.168.1.4's password:

Last login: Sat Jul 1 10:34:17 2017 from 192.168.1.2

The hostname is centos.localhost.localdomain
Hello today 's date is Sat Jul 1 10:35:52 IST 2017

3) Now, go to a non-login shell. For that merely, type **csh** and see what happens:

[jeff@centos ~] $ csh

The hostname is centos.localhost.localdomain

Only **.cshrc** is executed. The .login applies to the local shell, but .cshrc settings are valid across non-login shells as well. Also, remember that for non-login shells, the system wide files of **csh. login** and **csh. cshrc** (which reside in /etc directory) do not execute.

THE CSH.LOGIN AND CSH.CSHRC FILE FOR SYSTEM WIDE CUSTOMIZATION

The **csh.login** and **csh.cshrc** are not initialized for non-login shells. These files need Administrative privileges (login as root or in Ubuntu do a **sudo**), as is the norm for all configuration files that reside in **/etc** directory.

Let's look at the default permissions of **csh.login** and **csh.cshrc**

$ ls -l csh.*
-rw-r--r--. 1 root root 1602 Oct 15 2012 csh.cshrc
-rw-r--r--. 1 root root 794 Oct 15 2012 csh.login

Both the files are owned by the root and belong to the root group as well. The root user has read and write permissions on both **csh.cshrc** and **csh.login**. Both files contain lots of default settings, Paths and aliases. Create two variables in each file:

In **csh.cshrc**, go to the end of the file and add the following environment variable:

$ setenv CHECK cshrcCheck

When we login using jeff's credentials, this variable should be set because this is the default setting from the system-wide

csh.cshrc and is first read by the shell.

```
login as: jeff
jeff@192.168.1.4's password:
Access denied
jeff@192.168.1.4's password:
Last login: Sat Jul  1 10:35:51 2017 from 192.168.1.2
The hostname is centos.localhost.localdomain
Hello today 's date is  Sat Jul  1 15:48:42 IST 2017

[jeff@centos ~] $ echo $CHECK
cshrcCheck
```

Imagine the power of **csh.cshrc** if you have a large number of users. Just making changes in **csh.cshrc** impacts all the users. Use that power judiciously!

Since this an environment variable, even non-login shell inherits the variable:

```
[jeff@centos ~]$ csh
The hostname is centos.localhost.localdomain
[jeff@centos ~]$ echo $CHECK
cshrcCheck
```

CHAPTER 5: REGULAR EXPRESSIONS AND GREP, SED, FIND AND AWK

You may have heard lots of bad things about Regular Expressions, they are hard to learn, bizarre, confusing, takes years to master. And I am sorry to say that it is all true and more. But can you skip it? The Answer is a Big NO. But why? This is the age of automation, intelligent machines capable of making decision without human intervention. Data analysis is the byword nowadays, you should develop skills which are difficult to master. Because that's where the money is. There is nothing easy in this life and there are no shortcuts, unless your grandmother is the Queen of Great Britain!

Many of us were not particularly interested in Mathematics at school, but, Artificial Intelligence and Machine Learning is all about it!! Things we avoid earlier will come back to haunt us later. Karma or whatever you call it! Take this from a veteran of 22 years. Remember, like in exercise, no pain, no gain. Strive on...

META CHARACTERS

Are special characters used for pattern matching, commands employ them to perform actions on files or search for a pattern in inside a file. Meta characters play in important part in Regular expressions.

Meta Character	Action
* star	Matches Zero or more characters. It is a quantifier as well, because it means that an element preceding it can be matched zero or number of times.
? question mark	Matches exactly one character.
[ ] square brackets / parenthesis	Matches a single character inside the square brackets. Even if there is a range of characters in the inside the brackets, it will match any single character. For example, [ABC] will look at only match one character, it A or B or C (and not small a, b or c). You can also negate the search, consider this example [^XYZ], will match a

	SINGLE character that is either not X, Y or Z. However, be prepared for anomalies like the grep command which MAY match every character in the brackets.
\ backslash	Invalidates the meaning of certain special characters. The technical term is "escaping" character. Backslash is also used to match any character that follows it. Yes, backslash has a dual purpose.
^ It is spelt as CARET	Is a placeholder (anchor) indicating the start of a line
$ Dollar sign	Is a placeholder indicating the end of the line
. dot or period	Matches any character, it is a matching symbol.
| pipe	Matches characters EITHER to its left or right.

Table B, List of Meta Characters to memorize

GREP COMMAND

Grep stands for Global Regular Expression Print, it searches patterns in the files and prints out the output. The standard output is the name of the file, followed by a colon and the full line where it finds the expression. Grep has associate commands such as **fgrep** (fast grep) and **egrep** (extended grep) , while the former supports no regular expression the latter supports most of them, while grep supports limited number of regular expressions.

Create a file whose contents are files/directories of the etc directory:

$ ls /etc > etcfiles.txt

The pattern that you want to search should be enclosed within single quotes.

Now, search for all the files that begin with 'e' in the file etcfiles.txt

$ grep 'e' etcfiles.txt | more

a2ps-site.cfg
adjtime
aliases
aliases.d
aliases.db
aliases.YaST2save

alternatives
asound.state

And so on.....

But this is not the result I am looking for, grep has found all patterns that had **e** anywhere, whilst the requirement was to patterns that begin with **e**. To narrow down the result, use anchors. The two most popular anchors, for searching a pattern that occurs at the beginning and the ending of a line are ^ and $ respectively.

$ grep '^e' etcfiles.txt

enscript.cfg
environment
esd.conf
ethers
exports

The result is so efficient. Let's look for files that end with **f**. Now, **f** was not chosen randomly, but because **etc** contains many configuration files for daemons, services, protocols that have configuration files with **.conf** extension.

$ grep 'f$' etcfiles.txt

autofs_ldap_auth.conf
blkid.conf
dhclient6.conf
dhclient.conf
dnsmasq.conf
esd.conf
gai.conf
gconf
gnome_defaults.conf
grub.conf
gssapi_mech.conf
host.conf
idmapd.conf

idnalias.conf
idn.conf

And so on...

Another popular option is **-i** which is turns off case – sensitivity. You should use it by default. Consider this file. This file contains names with random numbers masquerading as telephone numbers

$ cat tele.txt

Jeff Jones +44-7840-947848-99

Pratim (773)-838-9835

Bobby Ha 9(87)8-80736-9302

Sujata Biswas +91-93993-97628

Pratim +888-93930-939, +888(9)-93993-93993

David Smith +(0)00093-9939-00002616-883

Grepping for Jeff returns nothing, because Linux is case-sensitive.

$ grep 'jeff' tele.txt

$

You can use the title case, but if it were a large file, you may not remember if Jeff was written in title case, using it with **-i** option gives you the correct result.

$ grep -i 'jeff' tele.txt

Jeff Jones +44-7840-947848-99

If you want to list records (rows), where **Jeff** doesn't occur, use the **-v** option which is like NOT. So using **-v** will show all the records excluding **Jeff**:

$ grep -iv 'jeff' tele.txt

$ grep -iv 'jeff' tele.txt

Pratim (773)-838-9835

Bobby Ha 9(87)8-80736-9302

Sujata Biswas +91-93993-97628

Pratim +888-93930-939, +888(9)-93993-93993

David Smith +(0)00093-9939-00002616-883

So now you see all the entries apart from Jeff's. Let's try using regular expression, in the **tele.txt** file, let's try to isolate Pratim's phone. How do we hone on to Pratim's phone number out of the other numbers will be your next challenge? Here, we need to call the option **-E** which supports Extended Regular expressions.

Note: Consult the manual page off Grep, you would find options such -G for basic regular expressions, or if you know Perl, you can use the -P option.

Of course, we can grep on Pratim and may get the result we want, but the challenge is to get it using Pratim's phone number.

Let's look at Pratim's number **(773)-838-9835**

It starts with a

- Opening Parenthesis
- Three Numbers
- Closing Parenthesis
- Dash
- Three numbers
- Dash
- Four Numbers

Note: Parentheses and Dash are metacharacters, which have special meaning to the shell, hence, must be "escaped" to get rid of their special meaning.

The **(773)-838-9835** can be represented by escaping the opening parenthesis which needs to be escaped, followed by three numerical values in the range, escaped closing parenthesis, an escaped dash, another three numbers, escaped dash and again a range of three numbers.

$ **grep -E '\([0-9][0-9][0-9]\)\-[0-9][0-9][0-9]\-[0-9][0-9][0-9][0-9]' tele.txt**

Pratim (773)-838-9835

However, this example is a bit complex, but good for practice, now, the range of [0-9] can be followed by curly braces with the 3 number inside. {3} specifies that the [0-9] will have three instances. Since, the last set contains 4 digits, the instance will be {4}

$ **grep -E '\([0-9]{3}\)\-[0-9]{3}\-[0-9]{4}' tele.txt**

And we get the same result.

Now, let's use grep on email addresses, let's use this file which contains some random email addresses, however, two of the addresses are not correct email addresses.

origae@david.com
dasrhinegold#bill.com
xeno@morph,com
terraform@mars.mil
ajsfkljasklf@ljsfl.org

Again, you will use **-E** option to get the Extended Regular expression. The first task will be to get the correct email addresses only and the second task will be getting the incorrect ones.

Getting the valid email addresses:

$ grep -E '^[a-z].*@.*\.(com|mil|org)' email.txt

Gives you the following result:

origae@david.com
terraform@mars.mil
ajsfkljasklf@ljsfl.org

^ was used because it is the beginning of the line. This is a place holder or the anchor.

[a-z] matches any one character

. period, here, means that it matches any character (apart from a newline character – not relevant here).

The * character means that any character that precedes it, can occur Zero or any number of times. Thus it, sort of, enables the. (period) or any character that dot matches to occur Zero or many times.

The @ is not a meta character and does not need escaping. Again, a combination of dot and star followed by dot – which needs escaping because it occurs before a com, org or mil in an email address.

You need the place the piping in a parenthesis because you want this grep with regular expression to give you all the valid domain names.

Getting the invalid email addresses:

Is very easy, if you employ the -v option which we studied earlier that reverses the meaning of the regular expression.

$ grep -Ev '^[a-z].*@.*\.(com|mil|org)' email.txt

**dasrhinegold#bill.com
xeno@morph,com**

THE SED COMMAND

Sed stands for steam editor. It is one of the three text manipulation commands in Linux along with **grep** and **awk**. A stream may be defined as a regular ASCII file. Standard input and output is a stream. Sed uses regular expression to find a stream of data and transforms into another data. Long story cut short, **sed** employs Regular expression to perform text substitution. The substitution command used with **sed** is **s** followed by delimiter forward slash, the pattern you want to replace, another slash, the replacement pattern and slash all enclosed inside single quotes.

sed 's/existing_pattern/replace_pattern/'

Let's look the following example, you know that if we echo a pattern, it is echoed back in the next prompt. The single quote is helpful and used so that the literal pattern is honored.

Look the following example and try to know the difference between using single and double quotes and the power of single quotes. These are little things which you can easily forget so it is worth a repeat.

- In this example, used, without any quotes, echoes the pattern.

%   echo SEA SHELL
SEA SHELL

- In the following example, putting **$** preceding **SHELL** allows variable expansion. $SHELL is an inbuilt variable which shows the shell you are in.

    % echo SEA $SHELL
    SEA /bin/csh

- Even if double quotes are used, variable expansion takes place, but what if you want the literal pattern to appear as it is, without variable expansion. Double quotes are unable to prevent the expansion of the variable.

    % echo "SEA $SHELL"
    SEA /bin/csh

- Now, you can see why single quotes are used, it turns off the special meaning of the dollar sign and treating it as other characters, so now, you get the literal phrase **SEA $SHELL**. Don't get confused. If you use single quotes it turns off the special meaning of **$** and treating it as a mere pattern. Remember literal with single quotes.

    % echo 'SEA $SHELL'
    SEA $SHELL

So, now you know why single quotes are in the substitution command of **sed**.

Now, for examples:

The **echo** returns the pattern Ursa Major and then using **sed** and substitution command **s** enclosed in single quotes you make the change. Also, you see the pipe symbol which passes the output of the echo command to **sed** to enable the substitution. The forward slash is the delimiter

$ echo 'Ursa Major'

Ursa Major

$ echo 'Ursa Major' | sed 's/Major/Minor/'

Ursa Minor

The **sed** command can also take other delimiters, but forward slash is the commonest. In the following example, comma is used as the delimiter. But, just stick to forward slash.

$ echo 'Sun has set'

Sun has set

$ echo 'Sun has set' | sed 's,Sun,Moon,'

Moon has set

Let's look at other examples of **sed**, consider the following file called **fruit.txt**, whose content is as follows:

Green pineapple
Green capsicum
Yellow pineapple
Yellow orange
Pink mango
Pink peach

The **sed** command changes all instances of **Yellow** to **Red**, however, the change is limited to the standard output. Nothing changes in the file.

$ cat fruits.txt

Green pineapple
Green capsicum
Yellow pineapple
Yellow orange
Pink mango
Pink peach

```
$ sed 's/Yellow/Red/' fruits.txt
```

Green pineapple
Green capsicum
Red pineapple
Red orange
Pink mango
Pink peach

You can use the **p** command to print out the altered lines, however, the output is not helpful, because **p** prints the altered lines twice. This is a natural behavior of the **p** command, because it streams and then prints every line, to suppress this, you need to use the **p** command in conjunction with the **n** command. The **-n** and **p** commands merit a different section, which will be covered as we go along.

```
$ sed 's/Yellow/Red/p' fruits.txt
```

Green pineapple
Green capsicum
Red pineapple
Red pineapple
Red orange
Red orange
Pink mango
Pink peach

To suppress the non-altered lines, use the **n** command as shown below:

```
$ sed -n 's/Yellow/Red/p' fruits.txt
```

Red pineapple
Red orange

This is helpful because it suppresses the non-altered lines and just prints the altered lines.

Let's work with another example to understand subexpressions in Regular expressions and its usage in **sed**. Subexpressions are a subset of Regular expressions and can be referred by a backlash. The subexpressions are put in the two brackets and then referred by number in the next part of the regular expression.

The example you will use is the file **months.txt**, the content of which is as follows:

$ cat months.txt

October
October
November
November

You can easily substitute October and November to December, but you can use it subtly as well to learn more about subexpressions and how it is anointed in the later part of the replacement sequence in **sed**.

Instead of changing October with December in one go, substitute the pattern "Octo" with "Decem", put the "ber" (here double quotes means nothing) between two parenthesis, this is a subexpression, and then, since it is the only subexpression in the command sequence refer to it as \1 in the next part and find out what happens

$ sed 's/Octo(ber)/Decem\1/' months.txt

sed: -e expression #1, char 20: invalid reference \1 on `s' command's RHS

However, you get an error. The error is because this is a Regular expression sequence and the parenthesis (or brackets) have a special meaning which is interpreted by the shell and hence you should escape them as follows:

```
$ sed 's/Octo\(ber\)/Decem\1/' months.txt
```
December
December
November
November

Note: Don't get confused, \(and \) have been escaped and the rest of the command really remains the same.

Now, there is **November** there as well in the **months.txt** file, if you need to make multiple substitutions (the correct phrase will be if you want to run multiple commands in a single **sed** sequence), you must use **-e** command to separate the commands:

```
$ sed -e 's/Octo\(ber\)/Decem\1/' -e 's/Novem\(ber\)/Decem\1/' months.txt
```

December
December
December
December

Note: The concepts may be hard to understand, you must put some effort and run examples of your own. Remember, these days organizations want you to bring all your skills apart from the kitchen sink.

The substitute command **s** can be applied to a line or a range of line numbers as well. You can see from the following example:

```
$ cat networking.txt
telnet
tracert
ping
sar
```

SUJATA BISWAS

uptime
uname

The **sar** command is mentioned in line number 4, you can address that in the **sed** along with **s** command, as you can see the 4th line has been substituted.

$ sed '4s/sar/vmstat/' networking.txt
telnet
tracert
ping
vmstat
uptime
uname

You can also use the **negation operator !** to apply substitution to all the lines barring a specified line number. Consider the following file, let's apply **sed** to change all the Month to capital letters barring the 4th line:

$ cat birthdays.txt
Month 01 Jan
Month 02 Feb
Month 03 Mar
Month 04 Apr
Month 05 May
Month 06 Jun

$ sed '4!s/Month/MONTH/' birthdays.txt

MONTH 01 Jan
MONTH 02 Feb
MONTH 03 Mar
Month 04 Apr
MONTH 05 May
MONTH 06 Jun

Pattern matching can also be used, consider the following file:

$ cat fileslines.txt

This is the first line
This is the second line
This is the third line

The pattern **This** is used to substitute **the** from lower to capital letters

$ sed '/This/s/the/THE/' fileslines.txt
This is THE first line
This is THE second line
This is THE third line

The -n and p command of sed

The **p** command of **sed** prints the lines twice, let's consider this file called filelines.txt

$ cat fileslines.txt

This is the first line
This is the second line
This is the third line
This is the fourth line
This is the fifth line
This is the sixth line
This is the seventh line
This is the eighth line
This is the ninth line
This is the tenth line
This is the eleventh line
This is the twelfth line

If you use the **p** (print) command, then the output is

$ **sed 'p' fileslines.txt**

This is the first line
This is the first line
This is the second line
This is the second line
This is the third line
This is the third line
This is the fourth line
This is the fourth line
This is the fifth line
This is the fifth line
This is the sixth line
This is the sixth line
This is the seventh line
This is the seventh line
This is the eighth line
This is the eighth line
This is the ninth line
This is the ninth line
This is the tenth line
This is the tenth line
This is the eleventh line
This is the eleventh line
This is the twelfth line
This is the twelfth line

As you can see, **p** prints the lines twice, once for output stream and another for printing. This behavior is suppressed by using -**n**

See the difference, that **-n** imparts

$ sed -n 'p' fileslines.txt

This is the first line
This is the second line
This is the third line
This is the fourth line
This is the fifth line
This is the sixth line
This is the seventh line
This is the eighth line
This is the ninth line
This is the tenth line
This is the eleventh line
This is the twelfth line

Using the **-n** and **p**, you can control which line you want to see, for instance, if you want to see only the 12th line, the command will be:

$ sed -n '12p' fileslines.txt

This is the twelfth line

You can specify a range as well, using the command in the following manner. In this example, lines 3 to 11 are shown.

$ sed -n '3,11p' fileslines.txt

This is the third line
This is the fourth line
This is the fifth line
This is the sixth line
This is the seventh line
This is the eighth line

SUJATA BISWAS

This is the ninth line
This is the tenth line
This is the eleventh line

Deletion using sed "d" command

Consider the file

$ cat fileslines.txt
This is the first line
This is the second line
This is the third line

To delete the 3rd line, the **d** should be used along with the line number, as in:

$ sed '3d' fileslines.txt
This is the first line
This is the second line

You can perform pattern based deletion as well, let's use the pattern first to delete the first line:

$ sed '/first/d' fileslines.txt
This is the second line
This is the third line

A useful regular expression that can be used with d is ^$ (the start and end placeholders/anchors) which deletes empty lines.

The following file contains empty lines now:
$ cat fileslines.txt
This is the first line

This is the second line

This is the third line

To delete the empty lines:

$ sed '/^$/d' fileslines.txt
This is the first line
This is the second line

SUJATA BISWAS

This is the third line

You can also use ^$ to delete unwanted headers from a file with line number followed by a comma:

$ sed '1,/^$/d' fileslines.txt

This is the second line

This is the third line

Note: ^$ will fail to delete those lines which appear empty but have had spaces or tabs in them.

ADDING A LINE USING SED'S A COMMAND

You can add a line using **sed's a** command, the command syntax is

sed '1a\ #Press ENTER here

> **content' <filename>**

1 is the line number.

Using the **fileslines.txt** again,

$ sed '4a
> This is fourth line' fileslines.txt
This is the first line

This is the second line

This is fourth line
This is the third line

Note: The command **a** adds a line after the specified number, that is, a line is added after the 4th line in this example.

The companion command for add **a** is **i for insertion:**

$ sed '2i\
> Hello How are you' fileslines.txt
This is the first line
Hello How are you

This is the second line

This is the third line

Note: The command **i** adds a line before the specified number, that is, a line is added after the 2nd line in this example.

Note: If you want to find the lines numbers in a long file, then you have use the = operator with **sed**:

$ sed '=' fileslines.txt
1
This is the first line
2

3
This is the second line
4

5
This is the third line
6

THE FIND COMMAND

The commands we are studying right now are very powerful, not only they drive your shell scripts, but also used extensively in System administration. The **find** is one such command.

As the name suggests it is used for finding files. The **find** command is used with the flag -name. Let's look at files ending with .sh extension in the /etc directory.

$ find . -name '*.sh'

The single dot stands for the current directory, and what is the current directory:

$ pwd

/etc

The current directory is **/etc**. Now, see the output of the find command, you should use the single quotes and wildcard character * (which has been covered in earlier sections). The find command searches recursively, meaning that it will search for files ending with **.sh** in the current directory, that is, /etc, and in the subdirectories of /etc as well.

$ find . -name '*.sh'

./bash_completion.d/gvfs-bash-completion.sh
find: `./lvm/archive': Permission denied
find: `./lvm/backup': Permission denied
find: `./lvm/cache': Permission denied

.

-

All you see is a single file found in the subdirectory of **/etc** called **bash_completion.d** and the rest of the files give "Permission Denied". This is because of permission issue, you should login as root to use the **find** command properly in system directories such as **/etc**. After using the **su** command to login as root, you get a clear output without Permission errors.

find . -name '*.sh'

./bash_completion.d/gvfs-bash-completion.sh
./vsftpd/vsftpd_conf_migrate.sh
./kde/env/gpg-agent-startup.sh
./kde/env/env.sh
./kde/env/ksshaskpass.sh
./kde/env/imsettings-kde.sh
./kde/shutdown/gpg-agent-shutdown.sh

There is another flag which is also commonly used and it is the **-type** and then you specify operators such as **f** for the file. There isn't any file called hello.d in the /etc directory, it was created to showcase the usage of the **find** command.

find . -type f -name '*.d'

./hello.d

If you remove the **-type f** flag, you get a whole bunch directories that end with **.d** extension. The directories with **.d** are mostly contain configuration files for daemons (a daemon is a background process).

find . -name '*.d'

./yum.repos.d
./bash_completion.d
./ggz.modules.d
./event.d
./libibverbs.d
./modprobe.d

./sudoers.d
./depmod.d
.
.
.

To search for directories only, use the syntax:

find . -type d -name '*.d'

A noteworthy usage of **find** is in the security sphere of System Administration, Linux Servers may be attacked by hackers and they look for files with all permissions (or the hacker may change the permissions to **777**). This permission gives all rights to the owner, to the group (users who are members of the group) and the whole world - read, write and execute permissions.

If you wish to practice this command, follow the steps:

- Create a directory in your HOME, say **find_practice**
- To create number of files quickly, use the command:

    $ touch {a..z}allpermissions.sh

Note: The touch either creates a new file or changes the access time of an existing file. **Go to the BASH shell to use this command, will not work in the C shell.**

- The special construct {a..z} will create files from aallpermissions.sh to zallpermissions.sh
- Give to give 777, use the command:

    $ chmod 777 [a-z]*

- Check the impact of the command on the files by entering the **ls -l** command

-rwxrwxrwx. 1 pratim test 0 Sep 5 00:09 aallpermissions.txt
-rwxrwxrwx. 1 pratim test 0 Sep 5 00:09 ballpermissions.txt
-rwxrwxrwx. 1 pratim test 0 Sep 5 00:09 callpermissions.txt

As you see, **-rwxrwxrwx** signifies that pratim, members of the group test and everyone else have Read, Write and Execute permissions on the files.

To list files for permissions, find has a flag called **-perm** and this is the syntax. Go up one level, that is, go back to your home directory from the sub directory **find_practice**.

$ pwd

/home/pratim/find_practice

$ cd

$ pwd

/home/pratim

Now, enter the following command:

$ find . -perm 777

./find_practice/qallpermissions.txt
./find_practice/lallpermissions.txt
./find_practice/tallpermissions.txt
./find_practice/sallpermissions.txt
./find_practice/xallpermissions.txt

The **find** command has found files with the insecure **777** permissions. You should now change the **777** permission to the safe **555**. Please note, this is a test environment, but in real life you may have **777** permission files in different directories. To change, the files to **555**, you will use **chmod 555** command, but imagine going into each directory and changing it, it will take a long time to finish this activity. But **find** command allows you the way to do it. At the same **find** command syntax, you can execute another Linux command that will act upon the output of the find command. The each output of the command is specified by {} and the flag used is -exec

$ find . -perm 777 -exec chmod 555 {} \;

The first part of the command **$ find . -perm 777** finds all the files with 777 permissions, as you have seen in the previous example.

The second part of the command, if you will, **-exec chmod 555** **{} \;** uses the exec flag to execute a Linux command **chmod 555** on the result gained out of the first part of the command. You have to use {} – which means that the chmod command is to be applied to each result (in this case, each file that has 777 permissions) and the syntax is closed by **\;**

Now, all the files that had 777 permissions have been changed to a safer 555 permissions, how do we verify that?

Running **$ find . -perm 777** yields no result.

But if you look for permissions with 555, you see the following result:

$ find . -perm 555

./find_practice/qallpermissions.txt
./find_practice/lallpermissions.txt
./find_practice/tallpermissions.txt
./find_practice/sallpermissions.txt

Just to make, sure, perform **ls -l** on any of the files and you see the change in permissions:

-r-xr-xr-x. 1 pratim test 0 Sep 5 00:09 aallpermissions.txt

As compared to previous:

-rwxrwxrwx. 1 pratim test 0 Sep 5 00:09 aallpermissions.txt

You can see that the **find** command can help protect, secure your system. Another option is the **-mtime**, using this flag you can find if any files have been modified. Hackers may compromise some system files so that they enter your environment. For instance, you make like to come on Monday and check if any system files have been modified in the last two days (weekend). Using the **-mtime** option and instead of . (period) , use / to signify all the files from the root for 2 days. You should login as root to avoid getting any permission denied errors.

find / -mtime +2 | less
/
/lib
/lib/libpthread-2.12.so
/lib/libss.so.2.0
/lib/libgio-2.0.so.0
/lib/libnss_dns-2.12.so
.
.

The output could be long, so it can be redirected to a file that you can study later.

find / -mtime +2 | less > changedin2days.log

If you want to find the access date of the files, that is, when the files were read, the example is:

find . -atime +20

The command finds all files accessed in the last 20 days in the current directory.

If an employee leaves your organization and you are tasked to delete her/his files from the system, this is how you will accomplish the job:

find /home -user pratim

If you are facing a space crunch or just need to spring clean your system by getting rid of large files, **find** offers locating files by their size. The option to use is, **-size** . This is followed by a suffix that represents file size notations such as shown in the table below:

Suffix	Definition
G	Gigabytes
M	Megabytes

| b | 512 bytes. This is the default. |

Table C

Create a big file by running this command, the **ls -lR** recursively checks all sub-directories of your system, which is then redirected to a file.

ls -lR / > filesize.example

The following command finds files that are 5 MB or more. The + sign indicates more.

find . -size +5M

./pratimb/Desktop/Python-3.3.3.tar
./pratimb/.mozilla/firefox/diegcd8q.default/places.sqlite
./filesize.example

You have got a nice list there, now, how about removing the files in one command. This is what System Administrators do, you should use the **-exec** flag that you studied earlier.

find . -size +5M -exec rm {} \;

find . -size +5M

#

The {} indicates the output to which the file removal command, **rm**, acts upon and when you run the command to find files of more than 5 MB again, it no longer displays the files it found earlier.

Practice the **find** command with emphasis on **-exec** flag, this is very useful for System Administrators.

THE AWK COMMAND

The main purpose of awk is generating formatted reports to meet business needs, from huge files by extracting useful bits of information. Your Sales/ Marketing or even your IT supervisor doesn't have time to go thru large files, instead it may be your responsibility to extract relevant information from such files. The **awk** is the tool you will use. Looking from an IT perspective, a certain TCP port which is listening for a background process (daemon) is not functioning properly. Instead of acknowledging the requests from clients, the port is seen to reject access. What should you do? You will contact your Network Administrator to send you a copy of firewall logs. Such logs can be of huge size and manually looking for the errant port may be next to impossible, but you can use **awk** to extract information whenever the port number appears in the log while at the same time filtering extraneous information.

While **awk** is like **sed**, that it allows parsing of records but it also supports conditions, functions and even scripting. AWK is named after its creators and is extensively used to format disparate pieces of data into tangible, reusable bits of information to fulfil business needs. It is a byword for text manipulation - which is composed of **records** or lines and in turn each line is divided into **fields**. Remember, the newer operating systems have gawk rather awk. That is, when you type awk it is gawk that executes. You may use the

$ man awk

$ man gawk

They both refer to the same content. The **g** in **gawk** stands for GNU -stands for GNU is not Unix.

Syntax of awk

The syntax is as follows:

awk options 'selection_conditions {command field_buffers}' input_file

- The awk takes input from the contents of the **input_file**.
- The **options** makes changes in the **command** behavior
- The **selection_conditions** may accommodate operators, functions, variables, programming logic and regular expressions, along with the **command** it is enclosed in single quotes.
- **Awk** operates on the **input_file** by reading one line at a time and applying commands to it.
- No changes are made in the original **input_file.**

EXAMPLES OF AWK

Look at the following file called **capitals.txt**, which contains the name of some countries followed by their capitals. Remember, from the awk's perspective each line is divided into fields. So, the first line Canada Ottawa has two fields, and will be designated as field 1 which is Canada and field 2 is Ottawa. The input we talked earlier is, of course, the **capitals.txt** file.

$ cat capitals.txt

Canada Ottawa
Chad   N'Djamena
Chile   Santiago
China   Beijing
Senegal Dakar
Serbia Belgrade
Seychelles   Victoria
Sierra Leone Freetown
Singapore   Singapore
Slovakia   Bratislava
Slovenia   Ljubljana
Kenya Nairobi
Kosovo Pristina

The syntax of the **awk** command is simple enough, you execute the binary (awk) followed by a space and the **awk** program enclosed in single quotes. Why single quotes? Because some characters have special meaning to the shell and single quotes are needed to nullify them. After the first single quote, you have the first brace which tells **ask** that the command should relate to all the lines in the input (which tells **awk to** get it from the text file, which, in this case is **capitals.txt**), then, it is the print command followed by the fields with a closing brace and a single quote and the name of the text file.

For instance, if you want to print only the names of the capitals in the standard output, then the **awk** command is

$ awk '{print $2}' capitals.txt
Ottawa
N'Djamena
Santiago
Beijing
Dakar
Belgrade
Victoria
Leone
Singapore
Bratislava
Ljubljana
Nairobi
Pristina

Note: Because of the Braces, the **awk** applies and shows the second column of each line. Print displays it on the standard output. The $2 is the second field and since it applies (due to the braces) to all the lines, it becomes the second column.

Similarly, you can print only the names of the countries which is the first column.

```
$ awk '{print $1}' capitals.txt
Canada
Chad
Chile
China
Senegal
Serbia
Seychelles
Sierra
Singapore
Slovakia
Slovenia
Kenya
Kosovo
```

Suppose, you want the name of Capitals to appear first before the countries, the command will be

```
$ awk '{print $2, $1}' capitals.txt
```

Note: Unlike **sed**, doesn't print to the standard output, which is why **print** command is used

The comma indicates that the columns will be separated by a space, the output will be:

```
$ awk '{print $2, $1}' capitals.txt
Ottawa Canada
N'Djamena Chad
Santiago Chile
Beijing China
Dakar Senegal
Belgrade Serbia
Victoria Seychelles
```

SUJATA BISWAS

Leone Sierra
Singapore Singapore
Bratislava Slovakia
Ljubljana Slovenia
Nairobi Kenya
Pristina Kosovo

A note about the buffers

To **awk**, a file is an assortment of records and fields. Awk considers a line in a file as a record. Thus, a record may contain number of fields which are separated by whitespaces. The fields are sort of stored in field buffers, which are nothing but $ followed by the number. You are, by now, aware what is a field buffer. There is another buffer called the record buffer and it is simply $0 (whole content of the file). There is only record buffer available for a file. It holds the total sum of fields and lines. In the following example, you can see what it is:

$ awk '{print $0}' capitals.txt
Canada Ottawa
Chad   N'Djamena
Chile   Santiago
China   Beijing
Senegal Dakar
Serbia Belgrade
Seychelles   Victoria
Sierra Leone   Freetown
Singapore   Singapore
Slovakia   Bratislava
Slovenia   Ljubljana
Kenya Nairobi
Kosovo Pristina

Note: The record buffer is mostly used in **awk** scripting (**awk** has its own scripting language). You can get the same result by eliminating the record buffer as well, so **awk '{print}' capitals.txt** will work as well.

Note: Be it record buffer or the field numbers – they are all variables.

Using Selection conditions in awk

Let's use this file going forward as an example, and keep adding content to it to learn more about **awk**.

$ cat salary.txt

Geneva	SystemAdmin	Jeff	100000
Delhi	SystemAdmin	Pratim	50000
Mumbai	Webmaster	Susan	30000
Washington	SystemAnalyst	Maurice	50000
Beijing	Webmaster	Alec	90000
Tokyo	Manager	Clive	100000
Seoul	Srmanager	Morgan	100000
Melbourne	DatabaseAdmin	Kitty	67000
Kolkata	NetworkAdmin	Elio	78000
Jakarta	SrNetworkAdmin	Oliver	98000
Delhi	PropertyAdmin	Raj	90000
Tokyo	PropertyAdmin	Pizu	89000

If you want to know the salary of System Administrators in the **salary.txt**, then you can employ a selection condition as shown below:

$ awk '/SystemAdmin/{print}' salary.txt
Geneva   SystemAdmin   Jeff   100000
Delhi   SystemAdmin   Pratim 50000

The selection condition is /SystemAdmin/ .

Note: The print command is considered by default, hence, this will work too –

awk '/SystemAdmin/' salary.txt

$NF and other variables in awk

Like $1, $2 fields, there is the $NF field buffer as well. This is the last field. You may like to find out the last field of an input file without referring to a number, this is, indeed, very helpful. Let's see how it works in **salary.txt** input file.

$ awk '{print $NF}' salary.txt

100000
50000
30000
50000
90000
100000
100000
67000
78000
98000
90000
89000

So, it just prints the last column of the file. But its usage is in long files with multiple fields. Don't get confused by variable and buffer are interchangeable to some degree, both hold values.

NR is a built-in variable in **awk** that counts the number of records, applying it in the **salary.txt** file, we get the count of the number of records:

$ awk '{print NR, $0}' salary.txt

1 Geneva   SystemAdmin Jeff   100000
2 Delhi   SystemAdmin Pratim 50000
3 Mumbai   Webmaster   Susan 30000

4	Washington	SystemAnalyst	Maurice	50000
5	Beijing	Webmaster	Alec	90000
6	Tokyo	Manager	Clive	100000
7	Seoul	Srmanager	Morgan	100000
8	Melbourne	DatabaseAdmin	Kitty	67000
9	Kolkata	NetworkAdmin	Elio	78000
10	Jakarta	SrNetworkAdmin	Oliver	98000
11	Delhi	PropertyAdmin	Raj	90000
12	Tokyo	PropertyAdmin	Pizu	89000

You can, as you have already seen, apply NR in the selection conditions of an **awk** command. To refresh your memory, the syntax of **awk** again:

awk options 'selection_conditions {command field_buffers}' input_file

If you want to see range of lines (or record numbers) then you can use NR in **awk**. The following command will show lines from 3 to 6

$ awk 'NR==3,NR==6{print NR, $0}' salary.txt

You can also it with patter matching, like get all records for Property Administrators, the command that you will use is:

$ awk '/PropertyAdmin/{print NR, $0}' salary.txt

| 11 Delhi | PropertyAdmin | Raj | 90000 |
| 12 Tokyo | PropertyAdmin | Pizu | 89000 |

Simple formatting

You can write simple text messages in the command area of **awk** to format the data presented to standard output.

For example, take the first record the salary.txt file, which is

Geneva   SystemAdmin   Jeff   100000

You may like to present in a way that is more understandable such as :

Jeff works in Geneva as SystemAdmin drawing a salary of 100000 US dollars

Imagine typing it for all the lines in the input file, instead awk offers a simple formatting procedure, which is

$ awk '{print $3, "works in", $1, "as", $2, "drawing a salary of", $NF, "US dollars"}' salary.txt

Jeff works in Geneva as SystemAdmin drawing a salary of 100000 US dollars
Pratim works in Delhi as SystemAdmin drawing a salary of 50000 US dollars
Susan works in Mumbai as Webmaster drawing a salary of 30000 US dollars
Maurice works in Washington as SystemAnalyst drawing a salary of 50000 US dollars
Alec works in Beijing as Webmaster drawing a salary of 90000 US dollars
Clive works in Tokyo as Manager drawing a salary of 100000 US dollars
Morgan works in Seoul as Srmanager drawing a salary of 100000 US dollars

Kitty works in Melbourne as DatabaseAdmin drawing a salary of 67000 US dollars
Elio works in Kolkata as NetworkAdmin drawing a salary of 78000 US dollars
Oliver works in Jakarta as SrNetworkAdmin drawing a salary of 98000 US dollars
Raj works in Delhi as PropertyAdmin drawing a salary of 90000 US dollars
Pizu works in Tokyo as PropertyAdmin drawing a salary of 89000 US dollars
works in as drawing a salary of US dollars

Now, note that in the previous output there is a dangling line occurrence:

works in as drawing a salary of US dollars

This is not wanted, to remove it from the output, you should employ NR built-in variable. NR stands for number of records in the input file and can be used to remove such danglers using != NOT EQUAL operator. The dangling line occurs at the 13th line and when we use the selection condition NR!=13, it removes the 13th line from the output, this is how you will use it:

$ awk 'NR!=13 {print $3, "works in", $1, "as", $2, "drawing a salary of", $4, "US dollars" }' salary1.txt

However, real life, as we all know, is full of unpleasant surprises and input files are no exception, there will be few files which will have whitespaces (or tabs) placed so that you can extract data using **awk**. There could be files that have commas, or bars separating the fields in the line (record). For instance, a snippet of the **salary.txt** file, you can create another file that looks like:

$ cat salary1.txt

Geneva,SystemAdmin,Jeff,10000

Delhi,SystemAdmin,Pratim,50000
Mumbai,Webmaster,Susan,30000

Since, awk considers whitespaces as delimiter, whereas, here you see commas as being field separators. Let's see who **awk** reacts to the change, we you try to print the second column:

$ awk '{print $2}' salary1.txt

$

The result is nothing, you don't see anything on the screen. But there is a way, using the -F option followed by the field separator.

$ awk -F',' '{print $2}' salary1.txt

SystemAdmin
SystemAdmin
Webmaster

Now, you see the correct result.

Combining commands

You can use the semicolon to have multiple commands. In this scenario, the company has decided to give a bonus of One thousand dollars on top of their salaries.

Using the **salary.txt**, create a new file with the following command:

$ cat bonus.txt
SystemAdmin Jeff 100000
SystemAdmin Pratim 50000
Webmaster Susan 30000
SystemAnalyst Maurice 50000
Webmaster Alec 90000
Manager Clive 100000
Srmanager Morgan 100000
DatabaseAdmin Kitty 67000
NetworkAdmin Elio 78000
SrNetworkAdmin Oliver 98000
PropertyAdmin Raj 90000
PropertyAdmin Pizu 89000

To add the sum 1000 dollars, using the following command separated by semi-colon. The first command performs a simple mathematical operation of adding 300 with field 2 and the second command displays the whole file.

$ awk '{$3=$3+1000 ; print $0 }' bonus.txt

SystemAdmin Jeff 101000
SystemAdmin Pratim 51000
Webmaster Susan 31000
SystemAnalyst Maurice 51000
Webmaster Alec 91000

Manager Clive 101000
Srmanager Morgan 101000
DatabaseAdmin Kitty 68000
NetworkAdmin Elio 79000
SrNetworkAdmin Oliver 99000
PropertyAdmin Raj 91000
PropertyAdmin Pizu 90000

Now, suppose the bonus is limited to a particular designation, say, the System Administrator (System Admin) should get the bonus and not others, this is possible by using a selection criterion.

$ awk '/SystemAdmin/{$3=$3+1000 ; print $0 }' bonus.txt

SystemAdmin Jeff 101000
SystemAdmin Pratim 51000

As you can see, only two made it for the bonus.

You can also have different amounts of the bonus applied to designations. Let's try and accomplish that on the System Administrator, Webmaster and the Property Administrator designations, the command will look like

$ awk '/SystemAdmin/{$3=$3+1000} ; /Webmaster/{$3=$3+500} ; /PropertyAdmin/{$3=$3+200} ; { print $0 }' bonus.txt

SystemAdmin Jeff 101000
SystemAdmin Pratim 51000
Webmaster Susan 30500
SystemAnalyst Maurice 50000
Webmaster Alec 90500
Manager Clive 100000
Srmanager Morgan 100000
DatabaseAdmin Kitty 67000
NetworkAdmin Elio 78000
SrNetworkAdmin Oliver 98000
PropertyAdmin Raj 90200
PropertyAdmin Pizu 89200

As you can see, Jeff and Pratim get 1000 added, Susan and Alec 500 and Raj and Pizu have 200 added to their salaries.

Awk Blocks

The blocks used in **awk** are BEGIN and END. The BEGIN block is used to initialize variables defined by you and put headings in the end output. Whereas the END block is where the **awk** processes the input file. A simplistic syntax will be:

$ awk 'BEGIN {command1 field_buffers} {command2 field_buffers}
END {command field_buffers}' input_file

Let us take the content of the file marks.txt to create a header and the footer. The header will be inserted by the BEGIN command (meaning before processing the input file, marks.txt), while the END command will after processing of the input file.

$ cat marks.txt

```
       Maths English Science
Rani   90    89      90
Pratim 70    69      78
Sujata 89    60      90
Bobby  88    90      100
```

$ awk 'BEGIN{print "Name of Students"} {print $0} END {print "End of report"}' marks.txt

```
Name of Students
       Maths English Science
Rani   90    89      90
Pratim 70    69      78
Sujata 89    60      90
```

Bobby 88 90 100

End of report

CHAPTER 6: ADVANCED TAKE ON SHELL FUNDAMENTALS

This chapter will consolidate all the stuff you have learnt in the preceding chapters. This chapter will dwell on the following topics:

VARIABLES

Variables are areas in Memory that store a temporary value. Many people, outside of IT, have trouble grasping this and confuse variables with files. Files take space on the hard disk, while a variable is associated with Memory.

There are two types of variables associated with the C shell:

1) User-created variables
2) Existing or Predefined Variables

USER-CREATED VARIABLES

As the name suggests, there are variables that you, the user, creates. There are some rules associated with variable creation that is followed by all programming languages. The variable must start with an alphabetical character, though under-bar/underscore is allowed.

If you try to start to create a variable starting with a number in C shell, in this case, 9, you get the following error:

$ setenv 9 100

setenv: Variable name must begin with a letter.

In Bash shell, the message is confusing as you can see from the message:

$ 9=100

bash: 9=100: command not found

However, underscore/under-bar is allowed, as you see from the following example:

$ setenv _9 100

$ echo $_9

100

Checking the value of **_9** using the **echo** command.

EXISTING OR PREDEFINED VARIABLES

The predefined variables are either shell (local) or environment (global) variables.

In C shell, the shell variable is set using the **set** command:

You simply assign a value to a variable, in this case, it is y and then check its value.

$ set y = 100

$ echo $y

100

If the value has a space or a special character than can get the shell confused, you must use double quotes. The dollar sign is needed before the variable to see its value using the **echo** command.

$ set x = "Hello World"

$ echo $x

Hello World

Using the variables x and y, you can employ it many ways, look at the example, in which variables y and x are used in the echo statement.

$ echo I shall count up to $y and then say $x
I shall count up to 100 and then say Hello World

Use the **unset** command to remove the variable.

$ unset x
$ echo $x
x: Undefined variable.

Some people use the concept of null value to a variable to unset it. Look at the set of following commands:

Setting n to 100

$ set n = 100

Checking the value of **n** variable

$ echo $n

100

Assigning a null value to **n**

$ set n =

Checking the value of n, you get nothing.

$ echo $n

Now, we come to an interesting of variables not only filenames and expansion using wildcard characters, but also storing the content of a file. Storing content of a file in a variable is useful in C Shell Case statement scripting.

To store multiple filenames in a variable with a wild card character, follow the steps:

Create multiple files using the command

$ touch file1 file2 file3 file4 file5

Check if the files have created.

$ ls -l
total 0

-rw-rw-r--. 1 pratim pratim 0 Oct 22 19:14 file1
-rw-rw-r--. 1 pratim pratim 0 Oct 22 19:14 file2
-rw-rw-r--. 1 pratim pratim 0 Oct 22 19:14 file3
-rw-rw-r--. 1 pratim pratim 0 Oct 22 19:14 file4
-rw-rw-r--. 1 pratim pratim 0 Oct 22 19:14 file5

Using the wildcard character for expansion and using double quotes assign the value to a variable called files and check its value.

$ set files = "file*"

Check the value of variable files

$ echo $files

file1 file2 file3 file4 file5

To submit the content of a file as a value to a variable, you need to use backquotes for command substitution and convert what you see on the screen into a string.

Create a file with the cat command, type the content and then press Control + d to save and exit.

$ cat > file1.txt

Hello, My name is Sujata

To see the value, you, can use the more command, like

$ more file1.txt

Hello, My name is Sujata

So, to put the content of **file1.txt** to a variable, using the following command:

$ set name = `more file1.txt`

And check the value

$ echo $name

Hello, My name is Sujata

Note: This is an important concept to learn, with little changes it applies to other scripting languages as well. Mostly used in processing and parsing of words. Imagine, that the content is a whole book and is assigned to a variable.

You can even store commands in a variable. However, the behavior of the C shell is such that complex commands may not work. Hence, it is better to use alias rather storing commands in a variable.

$ set x = `uptime`

$ echo $x

15:36:28 up 41 days, 22:49, 2 users, load average: 0.02, 0.01, 0.00

A variable (and its value) which is available in your current shell may not be available to its sub-shell. This is a relevant topic and worth repeating. Invariably, in shell scripting, a local variable is lost when another sub-shell (or child shell) is opened. Since, we have already touched upon this subject in C shell, let's try to understand it conceptually in BASH shell.

In the BASH shell, variable x is given the value of 100. This is your parent shell.

$ x=100

We check the value of x using the echo command.

$ echo $x

100

Open a sub-shell or child shell (this process is called **forking**), using the bash command

$ bash

Check the value of x variable, we get nothing. A blank space

$ echo $x

Type exit to go out of the child shell and return to the parent shell

$ exit

exit

We use the export command to make the variable available across sub-shells.

$ export x=200

We check the value.

$ echo $x

200

Opening a sub-shell.

$ bash

The sub-shell shows the same value. Thus, the variable has been successfully exported to different shells.

$ echo $x

200

It isn't mandatory to export variables; you just may need to work on the parent shell and not bother about whether the variable is available in sub-shells. For instance, you are troubleshooting a user's problem. So, what we have learned so far? We now know that there are TWO kinds of variables; exportable and non-exportable variables.

In C Shell:

You set a non-exportable variable using the **set** command. While, you set an exportable variable using the **setenv** command.

In Bash shell:

You set a non-exportable variable by simply using the following command syntax:

variable=value

To make it exportable, merely add the export command

$ export variable=value

Using **export** and **setenv** in bash and c shells respectively, whenever a new sub-shell is created, the variable gets formed in the sub-shell with the initial value (value set in the parent shell). You may change the value in the sub-shell, however, when you exit the sub-shell and get back to parent shell, the value is lost. Let's check this out:

In the C shell, create a variable called car to value kia

$ setenv car kia

Checking the value of car in the parent shell

$ echo $car

kia

Opening a sub-shell

$ csh

Checking the value of car, which is same as what it was in the parent shell

$ echo $car

kia

Changing the value of car to toyota in the sub-shell

$ setenv car toyota

Checking the new value in the sub-shell

$ echo $car

toyota

Exiting the sub-shell

$ exit

exit

Back, in the parent shell, the value changed in sub-shell is ignored and variable **car** reverts to the original value.

$ echo $car

kia

Environmental Variables

There is a quirkiness associated with environmental variables in C shell – the variables that determine and form your user environment. Variables in upper case are deemed exportable and those in lower case are not. But this is not very strictly reinforced in real-life production scenarios.

Some Environment Variables that you need to be aware of are:

Name of the Environment variable	Purpose
path / PATH	Contains list of directories where executables are searched for. You should check the value of the variable along with the **which** command. Note: It is better to use the small case **path** and set it using the **set** command. It is easier and almost industry standard.
SHELL	Check the value of the variable to find which shell you are using.
USER	Find your login name.
HOME	Your Home directory
MAIL	Identifies the location of your mailbox
HOSTNAME	The name of your system

Table D

The PATH/path environmental variable

When you type a command on the prompt in hopes of executing a command, the shell looks at the value of PATH/path variable to search for the command.

Look at the output of the following command, the value of PATH has /usr/lib/qt-3.3/bin, /usr/local/bin, /bin and /usr/bin directories.

$ echo $PATH

/usr/lib/qt-3.3/bin:/usr/local/bin:/bin:/usr/bin

So, when you execute the, say, **pwd** command, the shell look at the directories in the PATH variable and executes the command. But, how do we know that **pwd** is really is in the directories mentioned in the value of the PATH variable. This is done by using the **which** command:

$pwd

/home/pratim

The which is in the **/bin** directory as proven by the **which** command and so the shell is performing the search correctly. This is a real-life example.

$ which pwd

/bin/pwd

Let us create an executable file in /home/pratim and see how PATH, which behaves.

$ nano pathtest.sh

Content of path.sh

$ cat path.sh

echo "Hello All"

echo "BYE"

Giving executable permission to the user using the **chmod** command.

$ chmod u+x path.sh

Checking if the

$ ls -l pathtest.sh

-rwxrw-r--. 1 pratim pratim 41 Oct 29 16:45 pathtest.sh

How to execute the **pathtest.sh**? The pathtest.sh exists in /home/pratim directory which is not in PATH variable.

To execute an executable file which is not in the PATH variable, you MUST go to the location where the file exists and use ./ , which executes the command in the current directory.

Checking the location

$ pwd

/home/pratim

Despite the fact that you are in the directory where pathtest.sh exists, it fails to run. The reason? The /home/pratim is NOT in the PATH/path variable

$ pathtest.sh

pathtest.sh: Command not found.

To execute it from the current directory, use the following commands:

$ ./pathtest.sh

Hello All

BYE

$ sh pathtest.sh

Hello All

BYE

But what is the difference between **./** and **sh** ? They both help execute the executables from the current directory but **sh** forks out a new shell as well.

Now, you can put the /home/pratim in the PATH variable and check what happens:

The dot . is the symbol of the current directory and you have to save it from being misinterpreted by the shell using double quotes. The $PATH is the previous value of PATH variable.

$ setenv PATH $PATH":."

$ pathtest.sh

Hello All

BYE

Another example that will help you understand it better is. In this example, **/home/pratimb/vim1**, added after the original path.

$ setenv PATH $PATH":/home/pratimb/vim1"

Using the setenv PATH is rather unpredictable, what you can do is use the **set** command. And then put in the initialization file **.cshrc** so that the setting is read after the user logins.

The **set** syntax differs from **setenv** , so make sure that you practice it.

$ set path = ($path /home/pratimb/batch /home/pratim/dir1)

$ echo $path

/usr/lib/qt-3.3/bin /usr/local/bin /bin /usr/bin . /home/pratimb/vim1 /home/pratimb/vim1 /home/pratimb/batch /

home/pratim/dir1

Since, it is set on the current shell, as soon we log out, the value of the path will disappear as well. So, what you need to do is put in the **.cshrc** file. Log out and then login again to check the value of **$path** , then fork out another shell by typing **csh** and check if the path value is valid.

So, after making changes in the .cshrc file, which looks like:

$ cat .cshrc

set path = ($path /home/pratimb/batch /home/pratim/dir1)

Note: The default value of **.cshrc** is received by system-wide initialization file that you have learnt earlier about in the book.

After, you log in, the value of echo is same that we have set in **.cshrc**. The **$path** expands to the default value.

$ echo $path

/usr/lib/qt-3.3/bin /usr/local/bin /bin /usr/bin /home/pratimb/batch /home/pratim/dir1

Shell variable

The SHELL variable identifies the default shell of the user.

$ echo $SHELL

/bin/csh

User variable

The User variable identifies the username

$ echo $USER

pratim

You get the same output by using the **whoami** command.

$ whoami

pratim

Home variable

Home variable provides the path to your home directory. Many a Software may use this directory to store your files (that you create using the software).

$ echo $HOME

/home/pratim

Mail variable

As the name suggests, it identifies the directory to your mail box.

$ echo $MAIL

/var/spool/mail/pratim

Note: This output is from a Centos box.

Hostname variable

Identifies your hostname

$ echo $HOSTNAME

centos.localhost.localdomain

ALIASES

Aliases are commonly used in C shell environment, perhaps even more than in other shells. To find which aliases you have, type the command alias:

$ alias
l.   ls -d .* --color=auto
ll   ls -l --color=auto
ls   ls --color=auto
vi   vim

Aliases help you create customized commands that you can remember. If you are in the habit of going to a particular directory which has a long path name, you can have shortened version by using an alias. The syntax of the alias command is

alias <designation> <meaning>

Look at the following example in which a shortcut is created to know the Operating System of the machine:

$ alias osname 'cat /etc/redhat-release'

If you, now, type , osname, you get the following output:

$ osname

CentOS release 6.4 (Final)

If you run the command alias again, you will see that osname has been added to the list.

To remove the alias, enter the command **unalias** and the designation, the following example will do the trick:

$ unalias osname

To remove all aliases, enter the command:

$ unalias -a

Note: Do not try this command on productions machines.

VARIOUS OPTIONS OF ECHO COMMAND

The echo command is the shell's de facto standard output statement. When **echo** is followed by a variable or a string, it creates a file for the standard output that you see.

Example of a string:

$ echo "Hello, How are you?"

Hello, How are you?

Example of a variable:

$ echo $TERM

ansi

Be careful when you are using single quotes – which will not expand the variable or command's value. It will render the whole value into a literal string.

$ echo " The date is `date` "

The date is Mon Oct 30 18:48:14 IST 2017

Instead of using double quotes, use single quotes and see what happens:

$ echo ' The date is `date` '

The date is `date`

The single quotes didn't allow the execution of the date command. And the output is literal string. This is the job of single quotes.

The **echo** command supports many characters codes, the codes needs to be quotes, let's explore the most common ones with a single world example:

THE \B CHARACTER CODE - BACKSPACE

Originally

$ echo Hello World

Hello World

With **\b** in quotes, which is a backspace character, see how it eliminated the space after o of Hello. It has clubbed together the two words

$ echo Hello "\b"World

HelloWorld

THE -N SYNTAX – NO NEW LINE

Original

$ echo Hello World

Hello World

The last dollar sign is the prompt.

$ echo -n Hello World

Hello World$

Or

You can see the same behavior with **\c** character code:

$ echo Hello"\c"

Hello$

The tab \t character code:

The original is
$ echo Hello World
Hello World

With \b character code it looks like, notice the tab between Hello and World:

$ echo Hello"\t"World
Hello   World

THE FORM FEED \F CHARACTER CODE

The original is

$ echo Hello World

Hello World

Form feed means, using it just enables you to go to the next page. Not used much often.

$ echo Hello"\f"

Try it at your end, because it can't be represented here properly.

THE VERTICAL TAB \v CHARACTER CODE:

Original:

$ echo Hello World

Hello World

Using the vertical tab, changes the output quite a bit:

$ echo Hello"\v"World

Hello

    World

EXIT COMMAND

Used in shell scripting and in system administration, the exit status determines is the preceding command has been successful or not.

If you try to list a non-existent file with ls, for example:

$ ls pratim

ls: cannot access pratim: No such file or directory

Now, to check if the command is successful (obviously not) or not, check the values of either the **$?** Or **$status** variables.

$ ls pratim

ls: cannot access pratim: No such file or directory

$ echo $status

2

Note: You run the failed command again to get the exit value

$ ls pratim

ls: cannot access pratim: No such file or directory

$ echo $?

2

But, where do you find what is 2? What does 2 mean?

The way to do it to look at the man pages of ls:

```
$ man ls
```
And search for entries for the Exit Status. As per the man page entry in Centos, the meaning of 2 is

Exit status:

    0   if OK,

    1   if minor problems (e.g., cannot access subdirectory),

    2   if serious trouble (e.g., cannot access command-line argument).

Source: Man page of ls - snippet from Centos.

So, is the case with other Linux commands as well.

Let's see what happens if the file **pratim** does exist.

```
$ touch pratim
$ ls pratim
pratim
$ echo $?
0


$ ls pratim
pratim
$ echo $status
0
```

Both the variables show Zero, indicating that the preceding command is OK.

READING FROM THE COMMAND LINE

The variable construct to read input from the prompt in C shell is **$<** .

Let's explain with an example, set a variable to this construct using the **set** command

As soon as you set the variable name to the construct, and press Enter, an empty line is opened up, where you can type, say, a name and then check the value of the name

$ set name = $<

Jack

$ echo $name

Jack

It is not an efficient construct and can only take a single word without a space. This severely restricts its usage, unlike in the Bash shell, there is no built-in shell command like **read** in the C shell.

Let's see, use this construct in our first C shell script. Like the Bash Shell scripting, the first line in a C Shell is the command interpreter, which is **#!/bin/csh** and this you get by looking at the value of the Environment variable **SHELL**. Open your favorite editor, and type the following C shell script. Note, do not copy and paste, you will never learn this way. You must understand and type the scripts yourself. The Hard Way!

$ cat first.csh

#!/bin/csh

echo "Welcome to the New School Year"

echo "What is your name?"

set name = $<

echo "Thank you $name and Welcome to the School."

Explanation of the script **first.sh**

#!/bin/csh is the command interpreter and you have this line in every subsequent shell scripts that you create from now on.

echo "Welcome to the New School Year" Throws the phrase inside the double quotes to the standard output

echo "What is your name?" same as the preceding statement

set name = $< as this line is executed the shell waits for your input, which in this case, is, **Jack**. The variable name is assigned the value that you type.

echo "Thank you $name and Welcome to the School."** Prints the phrase and substitutes the value of **$name with its value, **Jack**.

To make the file executable:

$ chmod +x first.csh

To run the file from the current directory.

$ ./first.csh

$ ./first.csh

Welcome to the New School Year

What is your name?

#Waits

for input. Type, Jack

Jack

Thank you Jack and Welcome to the School.

Note: Most books recommend remarked comments, python groups make it sort of mandatory. In this book, you will not see much comments, because it becomes visually confusing. Do it in real-life, though.

POSITIONAL PARAMETERS IN C SHELL

The positional parameters are derived from the input that you enter. They are nine positional parameters, which are basically buffers (locations in your system's memory). These parameters are like variables used to make your C shell script more reusable.

Look at the following script, **second. csh**, carefully, there are three positional parameters **$argv[1] $argv[2], $argv[3]** so the entries you put in the prompt right after the script name correspond to it. The first entry is equivalent to **$argv[1]**, the first input becomes the value of the variable **$argv[1]**, the second input becomes the value of the variable **$argv[2]**, the third input to **$argv[3]**. The script merely opens and displays the contents the positional parameters when their values are files

$ cat second.csh

#!/bin/csh

cat $argv[1] $argv[2] $argv[3]

You can create three files which will act as inputs to the value of positional parameters. It is easier to use **cat > filename** to create files quickly for such tests.

```
$ cat first.txt
This is the first file
$ cat second.txt
This is the second file
$ cat third.txt
This is the third file
```

Now, run the script with the filenames as parameters which will be values for the arguments in the script file.

```
$ ./second.csh first.txt second.txt third.txt
```

```
$ ./second.csh first.txt second.txt third.txt
This is the first file
This is the second file
This is the third file
```

Roughly speaking the value of **argv[1]** is the content of **first.txt** which is in the first position and so on. What happens if we change the position numbers in **second.csh** file. The order/position of argv(s) have been changed.

```
$ cat second.csh
#!/bin/csh
cat $argv[2] $argv[3] $argv[1]
```

Will the position parameters adhere to the change? Will it be affixed to the position of the inputs? But as you can see **$argv[2]** is mapped to second.txt despite its input position of 2 while **$argv[2] is** placed first in the script file.

$ ./second.csh first.txt second.txt third.txt

This is the second file

This is the third file

This is the first file

This will take some time to understand, try to read this few times. This is an important concept and you need to understand it, positional arguments make scripts more widespread to use.

OPERATORS AND THEIR TYPES

One of the most important cog that runs the machine of shell scripting. The following topic should be at your fingerprints. Without mastery of this subject, you will find it difficult to write scripts, be it in C or BASH shell scripts; and will certainly help you in Python and other fancy (read "lucrative") languages. Reading off the screen won't help you, use pen and paper to practice and memorize, if need be.

There are four types of operators:
- Arithmetical operators
- Relational operators
- File testing operators
- Logical Operators

Arithmetical operators

Addition, subtraction, multiplication and division are operators that enable mathematical calculations that are used to calculate a value.

Arithmetical Operators in C shell:

Operators	Description
+	Used to calculate a value that is the sum of two numbers
-	Used to calculate a value that deducts the second number from the first
*	Multiplication of two numbers
/	Division
++	Incremental value, adds one to the variable.
--	Deducts the value of one from the variable.
=	Assignment operator

TABLE E

Caveats:
1) The data acted upon by the Operators must be numerical
2) The C shell looks at the numerical as strings. This poses a problem and requires the use of an arithmetic command represented by @.

$ set number=100

$ set add=$number+100

$ echo $add

100+100

Explanation:

A non-exportable variable **number** is assigned a value of 100. Then, we try to create another variable called **add** assigning it a value of **number** and adding it to 100 and hoping that **add** becomes 200. But, because the C shell sees "numerical" as character strings and merely echoes out a useless string **100+100**.

```
$ set number1=100
$ set number2=100
$ @ total = $number1 + $number2
$ echo $total
200
```

Explanation: Variables **number1** and **number2** are assigned values of 100. Using the **@** command they are added.

An important component of shell scripts that employ looping is incrementing a variable repeatedly till a certain condition is met. There is a prevailing propensity to suddenly introduce increment in the script without prior explanation. So, let's see how increment works:

```
$ set i=1
$ @ i++
$ echo $i
2
```

Explanation: The variable **i** is set 1 and adding the increment operator ++ you can achieve repeated looping with addition of 1 using **while** – which we will study later.

Mathematical operator +=

Mathematical operator += is useful as a counter, the application of which you will see in the last chapter of the book.

Consider the following example, in this example **x** is assigned a value of 100, the second line has **@** command followed += and 200, this adds 200 to the value of the variable **x**.

$ set x = 100

$ @ x += 200

$ echo $x

300

Relational operators

The relational operators compare two values to meet a condition of either False or True. These operators are a source of great confusion, so you may need to revise this section multiple times. The values that these operators can act upon are:

- Numerical
- Character Strings
- Patterns

Numerical

The operators applicable to Numerical values are:

Operator	Description
>	Greater Than
>=	Greater Than or equal
<	Lesser than
<=	Lesser than or equal
==	equal
!=	Not equal

TABLE F Relational Operators for Numerical Values

Character String

Operator	Description
==	Equal
!=	Not Equal

TABLE G Relational Operators for Character Strings

Patterns

Operator	Description
=~	Matches the pattern
!=	Not Matches the pattern

TABLE H Relational Operators for Patterns

File testing operators

File testing operators are used for determining the state of a file. Like, whether the file exists, readable, executable, writable. The condition to meet is TRUE, if not, it is FALSE.

Refer to the following table:

Operator	Description
-e filename	If the file exists, it is TRUE. If not, it is FALSE.
-r filename	If the file is readable, it is TRUE. If not, it is FALSE.
-l filename	If the file is a symbolic link, it is TRUE. If not, it is FALSE. Note: Read about the **ln** command.
-w filename	If the file is writable, it is TRUE. If not, it is FALSE.
-x filename	If the file is executable, it is TRUE. If not, it is FALSE.
-z filename	If the file is of ZERO bytes, it is TRUE. If not, it is FALSE.
-s filename	If the file exists and is greater than zero in size, it is TRUE or else FALSE
-d filename	If the file is a directory
-f filename	If the file exists and is an ordinary file, then it is TRUE or else FALSE.
-o filename	If the file is owned by the user, then it is TRUE or else FALSE.

TABLE I File operators

LOGICAL OPERATORS

C shell supports the following Logical Operators:

Operator	Symbol	Description
NOT	!	It makes a TRUE value into FALSE
AND	&&	Requires two Input Values, the result is TRUE only when the two input values are true. Otherwise, the result is always false.
OR	||	Requires two Input Values, the result is FALSE only when the two input values are FALSE. Otherwise, the result is always TRUE.

TABLE J Logical Operators.

Note: Logical Operators cannot be used with variables. But you can use them with Relational and File Operators. You will be extensively using them in shell scripting.

Logical Operators are rather difficult to understand without examples. Let's practice using the **test** command.

Create an empty directory in your HOME and **cd** to it:

$ test -f example1 && echo "The file does not exist"

$

Explanation:

The AND && requires that both the expressions, that is **test -f example1** and **echo "The file does not exist"** should be true. But since, we have just moved to a new created directory, it is empty. There is no file called **example1**. Automatically, the logical operator AND becomes FALSE and doesn't echo the message. Now, let's use the logical operator NOT before **-f example1**. What does it mean? The statement will now read as "test if the file **example1** does not exist". It doesn't. So, it is TRUE. The AND operator echoes the message "**The file does not exist**"

```
$ test ! -f example1 && echo "The file does not exist"
```
The file does not exist

Create a file using the **touch** command. The **touch** command always creates an empty file.

```
$ touch file1
$ ls -l
total 0
-rw-rw-r--. 1 pratim pratim 0 Nov  4 22:13 file1
```

Example:

Create a file called **file1** in your current directory, let's try the || (OR) operator, since it works on the premise of its expression being false.

```
$ ls -l
total 0
-rw-rw-r--. 1 pratim pratim 0 Nov  4 22:13 file1
```

The statement below reads that a file1 does NOT exist, because of the **! NOT** operator – which is FALSE and which is what makes the OR operator tick, which will go ahead and create a file called **Anotherfile**.

```
$ test ! -f file1 || touch AnotherFile
$ ls -l
total 0
-rw-rw-r--. 1 pratim pratim 0 Nov  4 23:04 AnotherFile
-rw-rw-r--. 1 pratim pratim 0 Nov  4 23:02 file1
```

CHAPTER 7: BEGINNING C SHELL SCRIPTING

The topics in this chapter will be:

- If-then-else: Decision Making
- Switch-Case Decisions
- Looping
- Parameters Again
- Troubleshooting C Shell Scripts
- Advanced Scripting and techniques

IF-THEN-ELSE: DECISION MAKING

This is a Decision-making flow that generally deals with two sets of data and accordingly decides the logic state of TRUE (zero) or FALSE (non-zero) and then, each would have its own set of outputs. Almost, all scripting and programming languages would have their own implementation of this greatly used decision mechanism varying only in the syntax.

SUPPORTED SYNTAXES OF IF-THEN-ELSE

In the following syntax, two expressions are evaluated and depending upon their state Zero or Non-Zero, different set of commands are executed.

if < the value is TRUE (zero)>

then

      \<execute command(s) if its TRUE>

else

      \<execute commands if its FALSE(non-zero)>

endif

But if you know, that the expression's value is true, but still want to automate the value of the expression, then you can go ahead and leave out the else statement.

if < the value is TRUE (zero) > then
      <execute command(s) >
endif

PUTTING COMMAND OUTPUTS INSIDE VARIABLES USING BACK TICKS

In shell scripting, it is common to put command outputs as values to variables which are then evaluated by If-then-else or case decision making scripts.

For example:

$ set host = `hostname`

$ echo $host

centos7

SCRIPTS

Script 1:

You can test if the file is readable or not. Refer to **TABLE I**.

Create a file called **readfoo.txt** using **touch** command:

$ ls -l

-rw-rw-r--. 1 jeff jeff 0 Nov 5 12:24 readfoo.txt

Remove the Read permission from **readfoo.txt** using the following command and again check with **ls -l**:

$ chmod -r readfoo.txt

Note: **chmod -r** removes READ permissions for members of the group and the whole world along with file's owner as well.

$ ls -l readfoo.txt

--w--w----. 1 jeff jeff 0 Nov 5 12:24 readfoo.txt

The script 1.sh

$ cat 1.sh

#!/bin/csh

if (-r $argv[1]) then

    echo "$argv[1] readable"

else

```
    echo " The file $argv[1] is not readable"
endif
```

The **$argv[1]** is the positional parameter that reads the first input after the script name. To run the script, make it executable using:

$ chmod u+x 1.sh

To run the script, you get an expected result because the file has no read permission.

$ ./1.sh readfoo.txt

The file readfoo.txt is not readable

Grant the file read permission using **chmod +r readfoo.txt** and run the script again.

$ ./1.sh readfoo.txt

readfoo.txt readable

This is how you test scripts, in Software Companies, product validation folks do this kind of job.

Script 2:

$ cat 2.sh

#!/bin/csh

if ($argv[1] =~ Hello) then

    echo " This is how you greet people"

else

    echo " You are wrong"

endif

The position parameter, **$argv[1]** matches a pattern **Hello** in the script and will return TRUE only if you type Hello right after the script. If you type anything else, it is deemed FALSE and the else statement comes into play and runs the echo "You are wrong" command. This is example of Pattern Matching.

$ ./2.csh Hello

This is how you greet people

$ ./2.csh Bye

You are wrong

Script 3:

```csh
#!/bin/csh
set cpu = `arch`
if ( $cpu =~ x86_64 ) then
        echo " This is a 64 bit machine"
else
        echo " This is a 32bit machine"
endif
```

Output of Linux command **arch** is a value for the variable called **cpu**. The output of **arch** is either x86_64 or i686, so you don't have to do any text manipulation. The output is pattern matched inside the script itself to x86_64 and it true prints the echo statement on the standard output.

$ ./3.csh

This is a 64 bit machine

Script 4:

$ cat 4.csh

#!/bin/csh

if (-e $argv[1] && -l $argv[1]) then

    echo " The file exists and is also a symlink"

else

    echo " The state of the file is not clear"

endif

Here is an example of an AND operator used with file operators that 1) checks for the existence of the file and 2) if the file is a symbolic link. For it to become TRUE both expressions must be true and then the statement **echo " The file exists and is also a symlink"** will be echoed. But if one of the expressions is false, that is, either the file doesn't exist, or even if it exists, is not a symlink, the logic becomes FALSE.

Create a regular file called **foosymlink.txt**

-rw-rw-r--. 1 jeff jeff   0 Nov 5 13:37 foosymlink.txt

And run it against this file:

$ ./4.csh foosymlink.txt

The state of the file is not clear

Now, create a symlink of **foosymlink.txt**, using the following command

$ ln -s foosymlink.txt fooYESsymlink.txt

A symlink differs from a regular file by the letter l in the permissions line of the file:

$ ls -l fooYESsymlink.txt

lrwxrwxrwx. 1 jeff jeff 14 Nov 5 13:39 fooYESsymlink.txt -> foosymlink.txt

Running, the file against the symlink satisfies the TRUE logic.

$ ./4.csh fooYESsymlink.txt

The file exists and is also a symlink

Script 5:

This is a system administration script which warns you about imminent disk full problem to a limit that is set by you. You will see the employment of various text manipulation commands that you have studied earlier. The target for disk space problem will be the boot partition. If you understand the script there is no need to read the detailed explanation that follows the script. This is also an example of nested loops, as you see the **else** is followed by another **if** statement.

```
$ cat 5.csh
#!/bin/csh
set boot = `df -k | awk '{print $6, $5}' | tail -n +3 | grep 'boot' | awk '{print $2}' | sed s/\%//g`
set spacelimit = 50
if ( $boot < $spacelimit ) then
        echo " The boot partition has enough space"
else
        if ( $boot >= $spacelimit ) then
        echo " WARNING, you are reaching the HALFWAY limit for boot. Please plan for more diskspace"

        endif
endif
```

Explanation:

To get the value of boot, run the **df -k** command on the prompt

```
$ df -k
Filesystem               1K-blocks   Used Available Use% Mounted on
/dev/mapper/centos_centos7-root       19085312    4240564
```

```
14844748 23% /
devtmpfs              497228     0  497228  0% /dev
tmpfs                            508116   0  508116  0% /
dev/shm
tmpfs                            508116 51632 456484 11% /run
tmpfs                            508116    0  508116  0% /sys/
fs/cgroup
/dev/sda1                       1038336 129780 908556 13% /
boot
```

Our target is the boot partition, you can see the 13% of the space allocated to it has been used. You need to remove all extraneous text to get this figure (13) as a value to the variable **boot**. The first **awk** prints out the 6th and 5th column, the **tail** command removes the header and another line below it, grep searches for the pattern boot, then the second **awk** command removes the first column and **sed** substitutes the % with a space to get 13. In the script, the **boot** variable gets the 13 as the current usage value. You then set another variable which is a limit for the boot partition. The first **if** statement checks the variables **boot** and **spacelimit**. If **boot** is less than **spacelimit** than everything is ok. You can change the value of **spacelimit** variable to say, 12, to make the script read the second nested looped **if** statement. This is an example of nested loop, check the employment two endif's.

$ ./5.csh

The boot partition has enough space

After changing the **spacelimit** variable inside the script, **5.csh**, to 12:

$ ./5.csh

WARNING, you are reaching the HALFWAY limit for boot. Please plan for more diskspace

Script 6:

This is a simple movie entry script that admits (or not) customers depending upon their age. It employs C shell's input grabber $< with mathematical operators of <= (Lesser than or equal) and >= Greater Than or equal. This script is also a nested loop.

```csh
$ cat 6.csh
#!/bin/csh
echo " Enter your age"
set age = $<

if ( $age <= 17 ) then
        echo "You are not eligible to watch this movie"
else
        if ( $age >= 18 ) then
        echo " You can watch this movie"
   endif
endif

$ ./6.csh
Enter your age
16
You are not eligible to watch this movie

$ ./6.csh
Enter your age
26
You can watch this movie
```

SWITCH-CASE DECISION

Decision through pattern matching is the goal of Switch-case decision shell scripts. In this shell script, a string is seemingly matched to multiple patterns. The **switch** statement ensures that the string is tested against each pattern and if there is a match, a code executed. If there is no match between the string and the pattern, the switch moves the string to the next pattern to match. If there is a match, the switch will terminate with the **endsw** command. If there is a match, other patterns are not checked.

The pattern is preceded by the **case** keyword and then ended by a colon. After the colon and in the next line there would be a command or set of commands. To make provision for the string that is not matching any of the case pattern, there is a **default** statement.

Syntax is

switch <string>
      case (Pattern 1):
      <command>
      case (Pattern 2):
      <command>
      case (Pattern 3):

    \<command\>
    default:
    \<command\>
endsw

Script 7:

$ cat 7.csh

#!/bin/csh

echo " Enter an alphabet between a to c in small letters:"

set alpha = $<

switch ($alpha)
    case a:
        echo "The upper case is A"
    case b:
        echo "The upper case is B"
    case c:
        echo "The upper case is C"
    default:
        echo " Enter only small letters between a and c"

endsw

Explanation:

$alpha is a variable that is coded to take a value that you input. You are only requested to input three letters in lower case, **a** or **b** or **c**. If you type **a**, switch matches the variable $alpha (that is value **a**) with the case statements. The case statement **case a** is a match; and the code **The upper case is A** is printed on the standard output. However, instead of terminating the script at this point, that is, switch should ideally end the script once a match is found, it goes on trying to find matches with other case statements and executing the codes. This is undesirable.

Check how depending upon the letter you enter, the output varies:

When you enter a, the codes analogous to **case b**, **case c** and **default** are executed. The default statement is a trash can of sorts, where inputs that doesn't make sense (or no match) to the script are dumped.

When you enter **a:**

$ ./7.csh

Enter an alphabet between a to c in small letters:

a

#The output where all the codes are executed.

The upper case is A

The upper case is B

The upper case is C

Enter only small letters between a and c

As you go down the script the number of codes that get executed get progressively smaller.

$ ./7.csh

Enter an alphabet between a to c in small letters:

b

The upper case is B

The upper case is C

Enter only small letters between a and c

$ ./7.csh

Enter an alphabet between a to c in small letters:

c

The upper case is C

Enter only small letters between a and c

$ ./7.csh

Enter an alphabet between a to c in small letters:

e

Enter only small letters between a and c

This is the reason breaksw is used after the case's statement code. When a match is found, breaksw gets the script to exit.

Script 8:

8.csh is the same script as 7.csh with **breaksw** that enables exiting of the script when a match is found.

```
$ cat 8.csh
#!/bin/csh

echo " Enter an alphabet between a to c  in small letters:"

set alpha = $<

switch ($alpha)
    case a:
        echo "The upper case is A"
        breaksw
    case b:
        echo "The upper case is B"
        breaksw
    case c:
        echo  "The upper case is C"
        breaksw
    default:
        echo " Enter only small letters between a and c"
        breaksw

endsw
```

Script 9:

In this example, if-then-else is combined with switch-case. The if-then-else statement is also nested loop script. The script also provided multiple choices in pattern matching used in one case statement.

$ cat 9.csh

```
#!/bin/csh
echo "Welcome to Magic Word Game, enter any alphabet between A to D \n"
echo "Enter the Alphabet:"
set a = $<
switch ($a)

    case [AabBcCdD]:
            if ($a == A) then
            echo "A stands for Apple"
            else
                if ($a == a) then
            echo "a stands for apricot"
            else
                if ($a == b) then
            echo "b stands for bread-fruit"
            else
                if ($a == B) then
            echo "B stands Blackberry"
            else
                if ($a == c) then
            echo "c stands for cherry"
```

```
        else
            if ($a == C) then
        echo "C stands for Coconut"
        else
            if ($a == d) then
        echo " d stands for dragon-fruit"
        else
            if ($a == D) then
        echo " D stands for Dewberries"

                    endif
                    endif
                    endif
                    endif
                    endif
                    endif
                    endif
            endif
        breaksw

    default:
            echo " Enter only alphabets between A and D"

endsw
```

Look at the long nested-loop if-then-else script embedded within a single case statement. In real life, you can expect such combination.

The **case [AabBcCdD]** is a construct that allows the choice of any single character within the brackets.

Script 10:

Imagine a scenario your software team has developed a prototype that has been complied in Centos 7.4 only and hasn't been tested on any other software. You are tasked to build a script that checks if the OS is 7.4. If not, give a message that the software can only be executed on Centos 7.4

$ cat 10.csh

#!/bin/csh

set os = `cat /etc/redhat-release | awk '{print $4}' | sed -r 's/.{5}$//'`

switch ($os)

    case 7.4:

        echo " You have Redhat edition $os which is supported by this software"

        breaksw

    default:

        echo " Only Centos 7.4 is supported by this software"

        breaksw

endsw

In this script, more than anything else, expect perhaps such scripts are routinely used in the software industry, it is the combination of **awk** and **sed** which is beneficial. While awk command is straightforward, sed uses the construct **sed -r 's/.{5}$//** to remove the last 5 characters from the output of

$ **cat /etc/redhat-release | awk '{print $4}'**

7.4.1708

The **sed** command is employed to remove the last 5 characters (including the dot), using the placeholder $ which acts on the last character of a line.

LOOPING

Looping refers to a programming concept in which an action is repeated till a condition is true, when the same condition becomes false, the loop is terminated. Another word for looping is iteration. The C shell has two looping mechanisms:

- While
- Foreach

WHILE LOOPING

In the while loop, the looping keeps on repeating until the condition is true. When the condition becomes false, the loop terminates. The premise must be that the condition must hold true in the beginning till the looping makes the condition false. The syntax of while loop is easier than in the Bash scripting.

Script 11:

$ cat 11.csh

#!/bin/csh

set i = 20

while ($i >= 10)

echo " Go to Mars"

@ i--

end

Now, if you are like me and had spent gazing out of the window during the Maths class you may find it difficult to understand the script. But here is the trick, consider at which stage this condition will become false

while ($i >= 10)

While **i** is less than or equal to **10**, the only number that fits the bill is **9**, since **i minus minus** (@ i--) will delete 1 number at time from the variable value **i** , the message "**Go to Mars**" will be repeated 11 times till the condition becomes false , that is, 9.

$ ./11.csh

Go to Mars

Go to Mars

Go to Mars

Go to Mars

Go to Mars

Go to Mars

Go to Mars

Go to Mars

Go to Mars

Go to Mars

Go to Mars

Script 12:

Assuredly, the following script can be written in other ways. But the point is that it can be written using a while loop. The problem is understanding the logic of while loop, hence, you must strive to spend time and write many seemingly simple scripts. You tend to forget looping very quickly so beware and book days learning the concepts which will help you learn other lucrative programming languages.

Here is a file checker script, checks if the file exists or not.

```
$ cat 12.csh
#!/bin/csh

echo "Enter the filename from your current directory: \n"
set x = $<
if ( -f $x ) then
      echo " $x exists"
else
      while ( ! -f $x )
      echo " There is no file called $x "
      exit 1
      end
endif
```

For a file that exists:

```
$ ls 3.csh
3.csh
```

Running the script

$ ./12.csh

Enter the filename from your current directory:

3.csh

3.csh exists

For a file that does not exist:

$ ls 14.csh

ls: cannot access 14.csh: No such file or directory

Running the script

$ ./12.csh

Enter the filename from your current directory:

14.csh

There is no file called 14.csh

Script 13:

$ cat 13.csh

#!/bin/csh

set i = 5

while ($i <= 10)

    echo "Now, Cassini is part of Saturn"

@ i++

end

Running the script:

$ 13.csh

Now, Cassini is part of Saturn
Now, Cassini is part of Saturn
Now, Cassini is part of Saturn
Now, Cassini is part of Saturn
Now, Cassini is part of Saturn
Now, Cassini is part of Saturn

Explanation:

What you should ask yourself is why did the script echoed the message **Now, Cassini is part of Saturn** six times.

As long as **i** is less or equal to 10, the while keeps on looping, adding an increment of 1 to 5, as soon as it reaches 11 which is not less or equal to 10, the loop is terminated.

Foreach looping

The foreach looping is a popular iteration technique and often used in the prompt itself. It consists of list of items, be it numerical, strings or even files. The looping depends on the number of items in the list.

Syntax:

foreach <variable> (item1 item2 item3)

    <code>

end

Script 14:

$ cat 14.csh

#!/bin/csh

foreach x (mango pineapple kiwi apple orange)

    echo "My favorite fruit is $x"

end

$ 14.csh

My favorite fruit is mango

My favorite fruit is pineapple

My favorite fruit is kiwi

My favorite fruit is apple

My favorite fruit is orange

Explanation:

The list contains five items, the iteration takes place 5 times as well. The code is **echo "My favorite fruit is $x"** is executed 5 times.

Script 15:

This is a more practical script, in which 4 IP (Internet Protocol) addresses are pinged. A possible scenario will be you are an IT personnel and diagnosing a user's computer which cannot connect to Internet. The four IP addresses you will likely to ping are:

127.0.0.1: This is called the Loopback address. Successful ping says that the TCP/IP (Transmission Control Protocol) stack is fine.

192.168.1.1: This is IP address of the gateway.

8.8.8.8 and 8.8.4.4: These are the Google's DNS (Domain Naming Scheme) protocols used for host to IP address translation.

```
$ cat 15.csh
#!/bin/csh
set x = "127.0.0.1 192.168.1.1 8.8.8.8 8.8.4.4"
foreach i ( $x )
        echo "_____"
        ping $i -c 1
        sleep 2
        echo " *************End*************"
end
```

Explanation:

A variable **x** is set valued to 3 IP addresses, protected by double quotes to avoid misinterpretation by the shell and the **foreach** loop mechanism. The **foreach** loop reads the value of x and puts it to variable i three times to execute the iteration.

Executing 15.csh

$ 15.csh

PING 127.0.0.1 (127.0.0.1) 56(84) bytes of data.

64 bytes from 127.0.0.1: icmp_seq=1 ttl=64 time=0.042 ms

--- 127.0.0.1 ping statistics ---

1 packets transmitted, 1 received, 0% packet loss, time 0ms

rtt min/avg/max/mdev = 0.042/0.042/0.042/0.000 ms

************End************

PING 192.168.1.1 (192.168.1.1) 56(84) bytes of data.

64 bytes from 192.168.1.1: icmp_seq=1 ttl=30 time=1.65 ms

--- 192.168.1.1 ping statistics ---

1 packets transmitted, 1 received, 0% packet loss, time 0ms

rtt min/avg/max/mdev = 1.655/1.655/1.655/0.000 ms

************End************

PING 8.8.8.8 (8.8.8.8) 56(84) bytes of data.

64 bytes from 8.8.8.8: icmp_seq=1 ttl=48 time=77.0 ms

--- 8.8.8.8 ping statistics ---

1 packets transmitted, 1 received, 0% packet loss, time 0ms
rtt min/avg/max/mdev = 77.039/77.039/77.039/0.000 ms
*************End*************

PING 8.8.4.4 (8.8.4.4) 56(84) bytes of data.
64 bytes from 8.8.4.4: icmp_seq=1 ttl=57 time=6.29 ms

--- 8.8.4.4 ping statistics ---
1 packets transmitted, 1 received, 0% packet loss, time 0ms
rtt min/avg/max/mdev = 6.296/6.296/6.296/0.000 ms
*************End*************

Script 16:

Using the arithmetic parameter @ in the following script:

```
$ cat 16.csh
#!/bin/csh
foreach i ( 100 500 600 700 800 850 900 )
        echo "$i X 1000 equals"
        @ total = ( $i * 1000 )
        echo $total
        sleep 2
end
```

Running the script:

```
$ 16.csh
100 X 1000 equals
100000
500 X 1000 equals
500000
600 X 1000 equals
600000
700 X 1000 equals
700000
800 X 1000 equals
800000
850 X 1000 equals
850000
900 X 1000 equals
900000
```

Script 17:

Use **foreach** loop to display the contents using the first parameter argv[1] – this will be name of a file. Create a file using

$ cat > hello.txt

Note: After typing, press Ctrl + d

Displaying the content of the file hello.txt

$ cat hello.txt

goodbye.txt

farewell.txt

Content of the script 17.csh

$ cat 17.csh

#!/bin/csh

foreach f ($argv[1])
      echo ""
      echo ""
      echo "The name of the file is $f"
      sleep 1
      echo ""
      echo "Displaying the content of $f"
      sleep 1
      head $f

end

Run the script with the name of the file.

$ 17.csh hello.txt

The name of the file is hello.txt

Displaying the content of hello.txt
goodbye.txt
farewell.txt

CHAPTER 8: ADVANCED TECHNIQUES AND SCRIPTING IN C SHELL

In this penultimate chapter, you shall revisit concepts that you have learnt earlier and learn new things, there will be emphasis on scripts that combine various techniques.

BREAK AND CONTINUE COMMAND:

The inbuilt commands used to while and **foreach** loops. **Break** is used to exit from the loop while **continue** returns to control to the condition statement. You can check the behavior of **break** and **continue** using **foreach** loop, which has five elements mars, saturn, pluto, ganymede, jupiter. Since Ganymede is a satellite it is the odd one out of the planets and will be used to demonstrate the break and continue commands.

Script 18.csh with Break

```
#!/bin/csh
foreach x ( mars saturn pluto ganymede jupiter )
        if ( $x =~ ganymede) then
                echo " ganymede is a satellite"
                break
        endif
        echo $x
end
```

In this example, **break** terminates the script as soon it encounters the Ganymede, when you run the script you get:

```
$ 18.csh
mars
saturn
pluto
ganymede is a satellite
```

However, Jupiter is not displayed with **break** command. Once the shell encounters **Break**, it takes the execution of the script to end.

Script 18a.csh with Continue

When continue is used in the same script as **18.csh**, the control goes back to the **foreach** expressions allowing the display of the fifth element in the list Jupiter.

```
#!/bin/csh
foreach x ( mars saturn pluto ganymede jupiter )
        if ( $x =~ ganymede) then
                echo " ganymede is a satellite"
                continue
        endif
        echo $x
end
```

When you execute the script, you get the following output:

```
$ 18a.csh
mars
saturn
pluto
ganymede is a satellite
jupiter
```

Once the shell encounters **Continue**, it takes the execution of the script to the **beginning of the script**.

REPEAT LOOPING:

A simple looping technique. You need to set a variable with a number loop iterations and call the variable while using the repeat loop as shown in the following example:

```
$ set loop_num = 10

$ repeat $loop_num echo Cassini
Cassini
Cassini
Cassini
Cassini
Cassini
Cassini
Cassini
Cassini
Cassini
Cassini

$ cat 19.csh
#!/bin/csh
set loop = 4
foreach i ( hello bye ciao )
        echo $i
        repeat $loop echo farewell
end
```

Can be used aesthetic purpose.

PARAMETERS AGAIN:

Besides the positional parameters argv[1], argv[2]... argv[9], there are three more parameters used in C shell that worth of special mention.

They are:
- Script name Identifier $0
- Parameter counter $#argv
- Parameter lister $argv

SCRIPT NAME IDENTIFIER $0

As you see from the following script, you need enter three arguments after the script name, which are **$argv[1] $argv[2] $argv[3]** and you display the name of the script by using **$0**. This is method is primary used to call other scripts and error handling because by using $0 you can easily identify if any script has failed.

```
$ cat 20.csh
#!/bin/csh
echo "These are positional parameters $argv[1] $argv[2] $argv[3]"
echo "The name of the script is: $0 \n"
```

Running the script with three arguments Tom, Dick and Harry:

```
$ 20.csh Tom Dick Harry
These are positional parameters Tom Dick Harry
The name of the script is: 20.csh
```

Parameter counter $#argv

This just keeps the number of arguments that you entered, you can use the earlier script with following edits:

```
$ cat 20a.csh
#!/bin/csh
echo "These are positional parameters $argv[1] $argv[2] $argv[3]"
echo "The name of the script is: $0 \n"
echo " The number of arguments that you entered after the script is $#argv "
```

Execute with the same arguments as before, check the last line.

```
$ 20a.csh Tom Dick Harry
These are positional parameters Tom Dick Harry
The name of the script is: 20a.csh
The number of arguments that you entered after the script is 3
```

PARAMETER LISTER $ARGV

This variable creates a list of arguments that you have entered, let's reuse the script used in last two sections. The last line has been added in the script.

$ cat 20b.csh
#!/bin/csh
echo "These are positional parameters $argv[1] $argv[2] $argv[3]"
echo "The name of the script is: $0 \n"
echo " The number of arguments that you entered after the script is $#argv "
echo " The list of arguments is $argv "

Running the script, look at the last line that lists the arguments.

$ 20b.csh Tom Dick Harry

These are positional parameters Tom Dick Harry

The name of the script is: 20b.csh

The number of arguments that you entered after the script is 3

The list of arguments is Tom Dick Harry

SHIFT COMMAND

There are only 9 position parameters allowed in C shell, from **argv[1]** to **argv[9]**, the way to extend its usage is by using the **shift** command, which moves parameters to the left.

Check the following script:

$ cat 21.csh

#!/bin/csh

while ($#argv > 0)

    echo $argv[1]

    echo ""

    sleep 1

    shift

end

The while loop is true till the parameter counter is more than zero. As the shift command shifts parameter values to the left, the count progressively decreases by one. When there are no parameter values left to process, the loop breaks. See, that only the first positional parameter **argv[1]** is mentioned because the shift command puts the successive parameter arguments to the first position till none is left.

To run the script:

$ 21.csh Tom Harry John Mary Bobby Subodh

Tom

Harry

John

Mary

Bobby

Subodh

INTRODUCING ARRAYS

An array is an indexed list of strings enclosed within brackets, the first value is referred to as Index1 and so on while the last value is referred by **$#arrayname**

To create an array list, use the set command:

$ set command_array = (ping telnet ssh tracert)

To see the content of the full array:

$ echo $command_array
ping telnet ssh tracert

To check the number of elements in the array:

$ echo $#command_array
4

To check the first element in the array:

$ echo $command_array[1]
Ping

To check the third element in the array:

$ echo $command_array[3]
ssh

To check the last element in the array (like when the list of values/elements is long):

$ echo $command_array[$#command_array]

tracert

CHAPTER 9
FREQUENTLY ASKED QUESTIONS

So, we have journeyed to the last chapter now. A look at Frequently Asked Questions on C Shell environment to tie up things together.

WHAT IS THE DIFFERENCE BETWEEN USING SOURCE COMMAND AND EXECUTING A SCRIPT NORMALLY?

When you execute a shell script in your current shell, it creates a child shell to execute in. After the execution is over and you are at the prompt again, you are back in the parent shell and all the settings of the child shell are forgotten.

In the production environment, source command is used to create an environment where you can run certain software temporarily, otherwise you can always put in the initialization file like **.cshrc**.

Let's consider the file **stest.csh**, such files contain setting environment variables and making changes in the path variable. For instance, you may execute a client application which, say, needs authentication from a TCP/IP service on a remote machine (192.168.1.1). The client software is available to the shell when you add its hierarchy to the path variable and knows the name of the remote server from an environment variable's value (in this case REMOTE_SERVER). Some software is specially programmed to look at a variable's value.

What is 8000? 8000 is the TCP port where the remote server's service listens for client requests.

```
$ cat stest.csh
#!/bin/csh
echo "Setting the value of the SERVER machine"
echo ""
set REMOTE_SERVER = 8000@192.168.1.1
sleep 2
echo ""
echo ""
echo 'Now changing the $path variable'
set path  = ( $path /home/jeff/source_test )
echo ""
echo "The New Path is:"
echo $path
```

Now, run this script like you execute an ordinary script by giving it executable permission and running it off the current shell.

```
$ ./stest.csh
Setting the value of the remote SERVER machine
8000@192.168.1.1
Now changing the $path variable
The New Path is:
/usr/local/bin /usr/bin /usr/local/sbin /usr/sbin . . /home/jeff/source_test
```

But, when you try to check the values nothing is set:

```
$ echo $REMOTE_SERVER
```
REMOTE_SERVER: Undefined variable.

```
$ echo $path
```
/usr/local/bin /usr/bin /usr/local/sbin /usr/sbin .

This proves that the script runs its own child shell and the values are lost when you get back to the parent shell.

So, what do we do to prevent from happening?

Yes, use the **source** command.

```
$ source stest.csh
```
Setting the value of the remote SERVER machine

8000@192.168.1.1

Now changing the $path variable

The New Path is:

/usr/local/bin /usr/bin /usr/local/sbin /usr/sbin . /home/jeff/source_test

Now, check the values of REMOTE_SERVER and path variables:

```
$ echo $REMOTE_SERVER
```
8000@192.168.1.1

```
$ echo $path
```
/usr/local/bin /usr/bin /usr/local/sbin /usr/sbin . /home/jeff/source_test

The values are intact in the parent shell after using **source**.

You can also use the initialization file **.cshrc** to make it quick changes in it and source it to test something on the fly instead of logging out and logging in again.

How can I initiate an infinite loop using "while" in BASH and C shells?

In C programming, the value ZERO is considered FALSE and any non-ZERO value is TRUE. This concept is used in C shell scripting as well.

To create an infinite loop in BASH shell:

$ cat while_infi_bash.sh

#!/bin/bash

while true

do

    echo "Hello Universe"

done

When you execute the script, Hello Universe will flood your screen and you can end the endless looping using Control + c. This is a cancel command and called SIGINT (interrupt signal). When you press Control + c, it sends an interrupt signal to the running process, in our case, the execution of **./while_infi_bash.sh** is stopped.

In C shell, instead of TRUE, 1 is used to signify TRUE, in the following manner:

```
$ cat while_infi.csh
#!/bin/csh
while (1)
      echo "Hello Universe"
end
```

Note: The syntax is much cleaner than BASH shell. To the point. You end the looping by using Control + C. It is used to create switch-case type of shell scripts.

Check this menu based script using while infinite loop:

```csh
$ cat test_infi.csh
#!/bin/csh
while (1)
echo " Main Menu"
echo "++++++++++++++++++++++++++++++++++++++++++"
echo "Press C to continue with the Script"
echo "Press B to exit out of the script ASAP"
echo "Press H to say Hello to the Universe"
echo "++++++++++++++++++++++++++++++++++++++++++"
    set x = $<
    if ( $x =~ [Cc] ) then
    continue
    endif
    if ( $x =~ [Bb] ) then
    break
    endif
    if ( $x =~ [Hh] ) then
    echo "Hello Universe"
    exit 0
end
```

Only when type C it goes to an infinite loop, while break command ensures the exit of the command as soon as you type B and the pressing H also leaves the script with exit 0.

What is the significance of exit 1, exit 2 and exit 3 etc. in the shell scripts?

Such exits are placeholders for the programmers to determine which part of the script has failed due to, say, an illegal input from a user. Taking the example from the last question, you see that three exits are added:

```csh
#!/bin/csh
while (1)
echo " Main Menu"
echo "++++++++++++++++++++++++++++++++++++++++++"
echo "Press C to exit with status 1"
echo "Press B to exit with status 2"
echo "Press H to exit with status 0"
echo "++++++++++++++++++++++++++++++++++++++++++"
    set x = $<
    if ( $x =~ [Cc] ) then
    exit 1
    endif
    if ( $x =~ [Bb] ) then
    exit 2
    endif
    if ( $x =~ [Hh] ) then
    echo "Hello Universe"
    exit 0
end
```

Execution of the scripts and exit with various statuses:

$ ./exit_test.csh

Main Menu

+++

Press C to exit with status 1

Press B to exit with status 2

Press H to exit with status 0

+++

C

Check the status by looking at the value of **$?**

$ echo $?

1

When **c** or **C** is selected, the script exits with status 1 as per the script. And this is applicable for **B** and **H** as well.

HOW DO I CONTROL AND VALIDATE INPUT OF ARGUMENTS TO THE SCRIPT?

You can't really control what the user inputs as arguments, but you need to anticipate so that your script comes up with an appropriate message and gets the script to exit cleanly. You need positional parameters in validating user arguments. The first step is to validate the number of parameters, which could be one or several. Even if your script needs several parameters for the user to input, there must be a bare minimum number without which the script should be designed to fail with an appropriate message. Hence, the first line of code needs to use Parameter Counter **$#argv**. The following examples are not really scripts per se, but lines of codes that you need to incorporate into your production scripts.

Example:

#!/bin/csh

if ($#argv != 2) then

```
        echo " The numbers of arguments allowed is 2 not $#argv
"
        exit 1
else
        echo "Hello $argv[1] and $argv[2]"
endif
```

Now, it is imperative to exact the operator != (not equal to) because the number of arguments has to be 2 not less not more. Hence, if the number of arguments is less than 2, the script will exit with an error condition of 1. Only if the number of arguments is 2 will the script work.

When the number of arguments is 1:

$ ./arg_checker.csh Tom

The numbers of arguments allowed is 2 not 1

When the number of arguments is more than 2:

$ ./arg_checker.csh Tom Harry John

The numbers of arguments allowed is 2 not 3

When the number of arguments is exactly 2:

$ ./arg_checker.csh Tom Harry

Hello Tom and Harry

Similarly, file validation is possible, look at the following script:

$ cat file_check.csh

```
#!/bin/csh
if ($#argv == 0) then
```

```
        echo "You can't have nothing in the argument, enter a file name"
        exit 1
endif
if (! -e $argv[1]) then
        echo "This file doesn't exist"
        exit 2
endif
if ( ! -w $argv[1] ) then
        echo " This file is not writable"
        exit 3
endif
if ( -e $argv[1] && -w $argv[1] ) then
        echo "The file $argv[1] exists and is also writable"
        exit 0
endif
```

There are 3 ways in which the script validates the file arguments.

If the user forgets to type the name of the file:

$ ./file_check.csh

You can't have nothing in the argument, enter a file name

If the user enters a file that doesn't yet exists

$ ./file_check.csh hello.txt

This file doesn't exist

If the file doesn't have write permission, for instance this file:

-r--r--r--. 1 jeff jeff   0 Nov 20 00:31 pratim.txt

All the write permissions were removed using **chmod -w pratim.txt** to enable this test.

$ ./file_check.csh pratim.txt

This file is not writable

HOW DO I TROUBLESHOOT MY C SHELL SCRIPTS?

To debug scripts in C shell environment, you can use the verbose option. You need to set it at the top of the script after the interpreter. Let's look at a script without and with verbose option set. This is a simple while loop which echoes 1 and 2.

```
$ cat debugging.csh
#!/bin/csh
set x = 1
while ( $x < 3 )
    echo $x
    @ x++
end
```

The output is 1 and 2.

Check the difference when verbose is added to the script:
```
#!/bin/csh
```

```
set verbose
set x = 1
while ( $x < 3 )
    echo $x
    @ x++
end
```

The output on the screen, extra debugging output is in Bold letters and the original output of 1 and 2 in normal. The loop keeps going on till the variable x is less than 3, when it is 3 due to the addition increment, the loop stops.

set x = 1
while ($x < 3)
echo $x
1
@ x++
end
while ($x < 3)
echo $x
2
@ x++
end
while ($x < 3)

IS IT POSSIBLE TO ACCOMPLISH FILE PARSING IN C SHELL SCRIPTS?

When the content of a file, say a text file, is broken into some parts and then analyzed - this is called parsing. You may perform parsing using arrays, which we've learnt earlier in the book. While you may wonder that a command like **wc -w** can achieve the same result of counting the words. This is about words in a file broken into individual components and acted upon and counted. This is a classic example, you may encounter while learning Python. Better to get concepts clear here – which is the aim of the book.

```
$ cat line_counter.csh
#!/bin/csh
set wordcounter = 0
set lines = `cat $argv[1]`
foreach words ($lines)
        @ wordcounter += $#words
end
```

echo "Total number of words: $wordcounter"

Explanation:
1) A variable **wordcounter** is set to Zero. As the name suggests it is meant to count the words in a file.
2) A variable **lines** is assigned the value of the first argument using **$argv[1]**. This will be the name of the file whose words you want to be counted.
3) A **foreach** loop is created where the variable **words** is assigned to each word in the file that you put in as the value of **$lines**. The expression **($line)** is an array.
4) The variable **wordcounter** which is assigned the value of Zero at the beginning of the script has the number of elements (of words) added to it by **$#words**. The **$#words** is, of course, the number of elements in the array.

This is the content of the file whose words will be counted:

$ cat ls.txt
hello10.txt
hello1.txt
hello2.txt
hello3.txt
hello4.txt
hello5.txt
hello6.txt
hello7.txt
hello8.txt
hello9.txt
line_counter.csh
ls.txt

$ wc -l ls.txt

12 ls.txt

We can use the **wc -w** command to know the number of words, which comes to be 12, let's check if the script gives the same value.

$ ./line_counter.csh ls.txt
Total number of words: 12